More responsive public services?

A guide to commissioning migrant and refugee community organisations

This publication can be provided in alternative formats, such as large print, Braille, audiotape and on disk.

Please contact:
Communications Department,
Joseph Rowntree Foundation,
The Homestead,
40 Water End,
York YO30 6WP.
Tel: 01904 615905.
Email: info@jrf.org.uk

More responsive public services?
A guide to commissioning migrant and refugee community organisations

Housing Associations' Charitable Trust

The **Joseph Rowntree Foundation** has supported this project as part of its programme of research and innovative development projects, which it hopes will be of value to policy makers, practitioners and service users. The facts presented and views expressed in this report are, however, those of the author[s] and not necessarily those of the Foundation.

Joseph Rowntree Foundation
The Homestead, 40 Water End, York YO30 6WP. Tel: 01904 629241
Website: www.jrf.org.uk

Housing Associations' Charitable Trust (hact) pioneers solutions to issues concerning people on the margins of mainstream housing provision. For further information on hact and its refugee housing integration programme please visit the website below.

hact
Octavia House, 50 Banner Street, London EC1Y 8ST. Tel: 020 7247 7800
Website: www.hact.org.uk

© Housing Associations' Charitable Trust 2008
First published 2008 by the Joseph Rowntree Foundation

All rights reserved. Reproduction of this report by photocopying or electronic means for non-commercial purposes is permitted. Otherwise, no part of this report may be reproduced, adapted, stored in a retrieval system or transmitted by any means, electronic, mechanical, photocopying, or otherwise without the prior written permission of the Joseph Rowntree Foundation.

ISBN: 978 1 85935 625 8 (paperback)
ISBN: 978 1 85935 626 5 (pdf)
A pdf version of this publication is available from the JRF website (www.jrf.org.uk). Further copies of this report, or any other JRF publication, can be obtained either from the JRF website (www.jrf.org.uk/bookshop/) or from our distributor, York Publishing Services (Tel: 01904 430033).

A CIP catalogue record for this report is available from the British Library.

Designed by Jeremy Spencer
Cover photograph by Paula Solloway. A Somalian refugee seeks advice at Trinity Resource Centre, part of hact's Birmingham Accommodate Project.
Printed by Genesis Print and Marketing

Examples of services included in this guide are given for illustration purposes only. Inclusion in the guide does **not** constitute an endorsement of any project or service, nor should the guide be cited as providing examples of 'good practice' where it refers to a particular project or service.

Hact and JRF are not responsible for the content or reliability of linked websites.

While every effort has been made to ensure the accuracy of information supplied, the publishers recommend all information be verified with relevant government agencies or other organisations referred to in the text.

Contents

Foreword by the Minister for the Third Sector … 9

Preface and Acknowledgements … 10

Glossary … 12

Chapter 1   Introduction … 13
- Why is this guide needed? … 13
- How does the guide relate to government policy? … 14
- Refugees and migrants – from service users to service providers? … 14
- What does the guide cover? … 15
- What does the guide aim to do? … 15
- Who is the guide for? … 16
- How was the guide prepared? … 17
- How is the guide organised? … 18
- Terms used in the guide … 18

PART ONE … 21

Chapter 2   MRCOs – the Background … 22
- Who and what are MRCOs? … 22
- How do MRCOs develop? … 23
- How do RCOs and MCOs differ from each other? … 24
- What is government policy towards the development of MRCOs? … 25
- What finance is available to help MRCOs develop? … 26
- What kinds of services do MRCOs provide? … 27
- MRCOs and Community Cohesion … 27

Chapter 3   Commissioning and Public Sector Reform … 30
- What are the 'agendas' for public sector reform? … 30
- What is commissioning about? … 31
- What are commissioning bodies looking for in service providers? … 32
- Commissioning and the 'efficiency' agenda … 37
- Commissioning and the 'modernisation' agenda for local government … 38
- How is local government responding to public sector reform? … 42

Chapter 4   What MRCOs can offer to Commissioning Bodies … 43
- What are the reasons for commissioning MRCOs as service providers? … 43
- How can MRCOs help to meet the objectives of delivering better services? … 44

	What is the 'third sector' agenda?	47
	How do MRCOs relate to the third sector agenda?	50
	What other 'carrots and sticks' exist to encourage commissioning bodies to engage with MRCOs?	50
Chapter 5	**Commissioned Services that MRCOs may Provide**	**56**
	What kinds of services?	56
	Accommodation and related services	57
	Services meeting immediate wider needs	57
	Services meeting longer-term needs	58
	Services meeting community-related needs	58
Chapter 6	**Providing Commissioned Services – Is it the Right Decision?**	**59**
	Is bidding to provide commissioned services a good idea?	59
	What basic questions do MRCOs need to ask themselves?	60
	How can MRCOs carry out this self-appraisal?	60
	Strategic questions about commissioning	63
	Opportunities and risks in providing commissioned services	64
Chapter 7	**Building MRCO Capacity to Deliver Commissioned Services**	**68**
	Why is capacity building important?	68
	How might MRCOs need to build their capacity?	70
	How can MRCOs build their capacity?	75
	Obtaining specialist help	76
	What help is available for capacity building?	80
	How do quality assurance systems relate to capacity building?	82
Chapter 8	**Commissioning Bodies' Role in Promoting MRCOs**	**85**
	How can commissioning bodies be more open to service provision by MRCOs?	85
	Are services appropriate for asylum seekers, refugees and new migrants?	86
	How can the commissioning process be made more accessible to MRCOs?	91
	What barriers might exist which discourage MRCOs?	93
	Can contracts be structured so as to give more opportunities to MRCOs?	96
	Running contracts in ways that help MRCO providers	98
Chapter 9	**Getting Started – What MRCOs can do to become Service Providers**	**100**
	Being aware of the market	100
	What is the MRCO's market position?	101
	Ways of entering the market	102
	Entering the market – a warning	104
	An overview of commissioning – typical steps	105
	Before making a bid	107
	Making a bid	107
	Delivering the contract	111

PART TWO — 113

Chapter 10 Accommodation and Related Services — 114
Who commissions accommodation services? — 114
What opportunities are there for bidding for commissioned services? — 115
Are there specific opportunities for third sector organisations? — 115
Are there examples of MRCOs providing commissioned accommodation services? — 115
What factors should MRCOs bear in mind and what requirements will they face? — 116
How can MRCOs find out more? — 117

Chapter 11 Providing Integration and Employment Services to Refugees — 118
What is the Refugee Integration and Employment Service? — 118
What opportunities are there for bidding for commissioned services? — 119
What potential exists for MRCOs? — 120
Are there examples of MRCOs providing Sunrise services? — 120
How can MRCOs find out more? — 121

Chapter 12 Housing-related Support through Supporting People — 122
What does Supporting People do? — 122
What opportunities are there for bidding for commissioned services? — 123
Are there specific opportunities for third sector organisations? — 124
Are there specific opportunities for BME organisations and for MRCOs? — 124
Examples of MRCOs providing SP services — 125
What factors should MRCOs bear in mind? — 126
What requirements will they face? — 126
Are changes likely in the near future? — 127
How can MRCOs find out more? — 128

Chapter 13 Improving Access to Healthcare — 129
Why do refugee and migrant communities find it difficult to access healthcare? — 129
Who is responsible for ensuring equality of access to healthcare? — 130
What is practice-based commissioning? — 131
Are there specific opportunities for third sector organisations? — 131
What potential exists for MRCOs? — 132
Some examples of services commissioned by NHS organisations — 133
What factors should MRCOs bear in mind? — 135
How can MRCOs find out more? — 136

Chapter 14 Legal Advice Services — 138
What are legal advice services? — 138
What opportunities are there for bidding for legal advice services? — 139
Are there specific opportunities for third sector organisations? — 141

	Are there specific opportunities for BME organisations?	142
	What potential exists for MRCOs?	142
	Are there examples of MRCOs providing legal advice services through contracts?	143
	What factors should MRCOs bear in mind?	144
	What requirements will they face?	145
	How can MRCOs find out more?	146
Chapter 15	**Helping Young People**	**147**
	What is Connexions?	147
	How does Connexions deliver services?	148
	How is Connexions developing?	150
	What opportunities are there for third sector and BME organisations, and for MRCOs?	150
	Are there examples of MRCOs providing Connexions services?	151
	What factors should MRCOs bear in mind and what requirements will they face?	152
	How can MRCOs find out more?	153
Chapter 16	**ESOL Training through the Learning and Skills Council**	**154**
	What does the Learning and Skills Council do?	154
	What opportunities are there for bidding for commissioned services?	155
	Are there specific opportunities for third sector organisations?	156
	Are there specific opportunities for MRCOs?	157
	Are there examples of MRCOs providing services to LSC?	158
	What factors should MRCOs bear in mind?	159
	What requirements will they face?	159
	How can MRCOs find out more?	160
Chapter 17	**Job-Related Training and Other Services through JCP**	**161**
	What is Jobcentre Plus and what services does it commission?	161
	Are there specific opportunities for third sector organisations?	162
	Are there specific opportunities for BME organisations and MRCOs?	162
	Are there examples of MRCOs providing services to JCP?	163
	What factors should MRCOs bear in mind?	164
	How can MRCOs find out more?	165
Appendix 1	Key Documents and Information Sources on Commissioning and MRCOs	167
Appendix 2	Sources of Help with Capacity Building	169

Foreword by the Minister for the Third Sector

This is an important guide whose themes are central to some of our country's biggest challenges today. How do we make sure everyone in Britain has the same chances to progress? How do we support *everyone* in taking up those chances and making the most of their opportunities? I believe the third sector, working in partnership with the public sector, has a vital role to play here.

The best third sector organisations supporting migrants and refugees encapsulate many of the strengths of the third sector as a whole. They are organisations which often grow out of the communities which they seek to serve. Organisations which can reach people who might be hidden from the traditional public service structures, and organisations which are trusted by those people.

I celebrate the contribution of many third sector organisations which work with migrants and refugees without any involvement from the public sector. But for those that do want to work with us, our ambition is to create an environment in which all sectors can play to their strengths.

This ambition brings significant opportunities for us all to work to improve services for migrants and refugees. It also brings a number of challenges for both the public sector and those third sector organisations which want to play a part.

For local public sector organisations, simply understanding the nature and scale of third sector organisations in their areas can often be a significant task in itself when the third sector's strength is in its variety. For the third sector, particularly smaller organisations like the majority of those working with migrants and refugees, starting to work with the public sector and understanding the new language of commissioning can often require a major culture change.

I therefore warmly welcome this new guide, which is designed in order to help both commissioners and third sector organisations navigate their way through this terrain. Ultimately, I hope it will contribute to better, more responsive public services for all refugees and migrants in Britain today and in the future.

Phil Hope

Phil Hope MP
Minister for the Third Sector

Preface and Acknowledgements

Hact pioneers housing solutions to problems facing our most marginalised communities. Forced migrants – or refugees – have figured prominently in hact's work since the late 1980s, and recently we extended our work to other new migrant groups.

The learning and trust that have developed from hact's work with migrant and refugee community organisations (MRCOs) are perhaps the reason that the Joseph Rowntree Foundation commissioned us to produce this guide. It covers accommodation, employment and training, services for young people, social care and housing-related support services. At its heart are the interests and aspirations of migrants and refugees. To address these needs, the guide explores the potential for co-operation between MRCOs and public commissioning bodies in improving services for some of our most hidden communities.

Underpinning the government's commitment to the third sector is a belief that engaging with voluntary and community organisations can improve equitable access, responsiveness, quality and diversity in provision of public services. This strategy could transform public services. And in an era of global migration, the involvement of MRCOs in the commissioning agenda creates formal links between public bodies and our new communities that could help to build an important sense of citizenship and belonging – going way beyond the provision of services.

This guide aims to contribute to this process of change. It is targeted at commissioners and MRCOs who wish to engage in developing services for the many new and diverse communities now settling in the UK. It outlines what commissioners and groups can do to establish direct contracting arrangements. It is also useful for those seeking to engage with each other so as to better understand needs, gaps in provision and the potential for developing other mechanisms for changing or developing services.

The need to invest in new communities to enable their meaningful engagement should not be underestimated. But it should be considered against the cost of wasted potential or the potential lack of preventative solutions that might otherwise be developed.

We are extremely grateful to the Joseph Rowntree Foundation for funding and publishing the guide, which is based on two years of research in England, Scotland and Wales. Hact would like to thank John Perry and A. Azim El-Hassan and the wide range of MRCOs, commissioners and national, regional and local partner agencies and individuals across the UK who have contributed to it through being interviewed, or by attending the seminars that were held in various parts of England, Wales and Scotland. Within hact itself, Mauro Tadiwe and Barbara Nea were particularly involved in ensuring this project had a successful outcome.

In addition to the two main researchers and writers, material was contributed by Michael Collins (Scotland) and Dewi Owen and Eid Ali Ahmed (Wales). Many more people made specialist contributions to part two of the guide, commented on drafts of the text or made presentations to the seminars. These included:

- Saeed Abdi, MAAN Somali Mental Health
- Fiona Aldridge, National Institute of Adult Continuing Education
- Mohamed Alsahimi, Arab Training and Information Centre
- Mohamed Arwo, Astonbrook Housing Association
- Dave Atkinson, Home Office
- Simin Azimi, Refugee Women's Association
- Jonathan Bailey, Department for Work and Pensions
- Peter Boileau, Care Services Improvement Partnership, West Midlands
- Diane Dixon, consultant
- Jonathan Ellis, Refugee Council
- Yohannes Fassil, consultant
- Naomi Hatton, Home Office
- Simon Hebditch, Capacitybuilders
- Pat Jones, CURS, University of Birmingham
- Judy Lowe, London Borough of Sutton (formerly of hact)
- Sue Lukes, hact associate and freelance consultant
- Tim Miller, Sheffield City Council
- Chetan Patel, Home Office
- Matthew Pelling, London Borough of Haringey
- Adrian Randall, Birmingham City Council
- Jim Steinke, Northern Refugee Centre
- Mulat Tadesse, Refugee Advice and Support Centre
- Cheryl Turner, Learning and Skills Council
- Juan Varela, Northern Refugee Centre
- Nigel Walker, Care Services Improvement Partnership
- Dick Williams, Refugee Council
- Liz Williams, Department for Work and Pensions
- Jon Williams, Senior LORECA Manager, London Development Agency
- Sarah Wood, Office of the Third Sector and IDeA

Heather Petch
Director, hact
February 2008

Glossary of acronyms used in the text

This includes those acronyms used throughout the text, but omits ones only used in a particular chapter or section.

BIA	Borders and Immigration Agency
BME	Black and Minority Ethnic
BV	best value
CAA	Comprehensive Area Assessment
CLG	Communities and Local Government (Department for)
CPA	Comprehensive Performance Assessment
DCSF	Department for Children, Schools and Families
DH	Department of Health
DWP	Department for Work and Pensions
ESOL	English for Speakers of Other Languages
hact	Housing Associations' Charitable Trust
ICT	Information and Communications Technology
JCP	Jobcentre Plus
JRF	Joseph Rowntree Foundation
LAA	Local Area Agreement
LGA	Local Government Association
LSC	Learning and Skills Council
LSP	Local Strategic Partnership
MCO	Migrant Community Organisation
MRCO	Migrant and Refugee Community Organisation
NCVO	National Council for Voluntary Organisations
NHS	National Health Service
OGC	Office of Government Commerce
OTS	Office of the Third Sector
PCT	Primary Care Trust
PSA	Public Service Agreement
RCO	Refugee Community Organisation
SP	Supporting People
VFM	value for money
WAG	Welsh Assembly Government

Chapter 1

Introduction

Why is this guide needed?

Migration is changing the face of Britain's population. It has accounted for about half of Britain's population growth in the last ten years. In the last five years, about 200,000 people have been accepted as refugees and are now settled in Britain on a long-term basis. Since enlargement of the European Union in May 2004, more than 400,000 people from the new EU states have registered for work in the UK (although many of these may be here only temporarily).

Many more nationalities are now well-represented in the UK population, alongside the established communities of people whose origins are in the 'New Commonwealth' countries. In 1981, Indian, Black Caribbean and Pakistani communities accounted for 63 per cent of the BME population. By 2003, this proportion had fallen to 49 per cent. Of the five million BME people in Britain, half were born abroad.[1]

There are new migrant communities emerging in many parts of the country that have few social or cultural similarities to longer-established BME groups. Many of these new communities have formed new organisations – often called refugee community organisations or migrant community organisations (in this guide, referred to collectively as MRCOs). They provide vital support services to their communities. But such services are often not part of any wider local or national structure for service provision. Several groups are now providing more fully developed services – and many more would like to do so. Among other benefits, being part of a formal structure enables groups both to improve the quality of their services, and to prove that they are doing so.

Becoming providers of publicly funded services may also have wider benefits in helping the integration of migrant communities. These communities are among the most isolated sections of society, whose needs are often unrecognised or underestimated by the formal public sector. By becoming providers of public services themselves, groups rooted in those communities can address neglected problems, reduce the isolation felt by society's 'newcomers' and at the same time help those public services meet more of the community's needs.

---

1 Figures in the opening paragraphs are taken from www.statistics.gov.uk or from the Born Abroad part of the BBC website (http://news.bbc.co.uk/). More detailed regional information can be obtained from the BBC site.

How does the guide relate to government policy?

Publicly funded support and advice services have a significant role in the economy, and form a substantial part of the activities of at least eight government departments, all local authorities and many other bodies such as Learning and Skills Councils. Many of these services are now 'commissioned' rather than being directly provided, and the proportion of services which are commissioned is set to grow. At the same time, it is also government policy to expand the role of the 'third sector' in providing these services. It defines the third sector as:[2]

> '...non-governmental organisations which are value-driven and which principally reinvest their surpluses to further social, environmental or cultural objectives. It includes voluntary and community organisations, charities, social enterprises, cooperatives and mutuals.'

The third sector already earns in excess of £12bn annually from selling its services, and nearly half of this income comes from selling services to government.[3]

Government policy also recognises the role that the third sector can play in *transforming the delivery* of these services – achieving greater value for money and providing services more appropriate to people's needs. The government wants to build the required skills among voluntary and community groups, so as to increase their role as service providers. This includes smaller bodies which are already providing community-based services: MRCOs should have the opportunity to be part of this larger reform.

Refugees and migrants – from service users to service providers?

Quite apart from the general growth in support and advice services, the needs of asylum seekers, refugees and migrants have led both to their needing access to such services, and to the development of specific services for them. There are now several funding streams directly aimed at their needs, or in which such needs have become a recognised service area. In addition, some bodies responsible for commissioning services – such as local authorities and Primary Care Trusts – have started to recognise and address the specific needs of migrant groups.

---

[2] HM Treasury (2007) *The Future Role of the Third Sector in Economic and Social Regeneration: Final Report*, p5.

[3] HM Treasury (2006) *The Future Role of the Third Sector in Economic and Social Regeneration: Interim Report*, p30.

But despite government commitment to the third sector, refugee and migrant organisations, as mainly small voluntary groups, still find many difficulties in being commissioned to *provide* such services. MRCOs are not necessarily recognised as potential service providers by commissioning bodies. Hence the need for this guide: it explains the greater role these groups could play, and how they could go about fulfilling it.

What does the guide cover?

The guide covers a comprehensive range of relevant services, including accommodation, training, legal advice, physical and mental health, and other support services. These are all areas of work in which migrant and refugee community organisations already play a part, and in which they hope to have a bigger role over the next few years.

The guide is about public services which are 'commissioned' from third parties (in this case, MRCOs) – normally through competition – and operated under legal contracts. It is *not* about grant-aid for MRCOs, whether for core costs or to provide particular services, although of course MRCOs who are commissioned to provide services may also be in receipt of grants for other aspects of their work.[4] (The ways that terms like 'commissioning' are used in the guide are defined at the end of this chapter.)

What does the guide aim to do?

The guide's main aim is to set out the case for MRCOs as providers of commissioned public services – both to show *commissioners* why they should consider them, and help *MRCOs* understand and form their own views on what their potential roles could be. In this respect the guide's aim is to change the climate of opinion – on both 'sides' of the commissioning process – as well as to show how such a change fits in with wider government reform of the public services.

Of course there is already a range of advice available about the role of third sector organisations as service providers, and some of this is aimed at black and minority ethnic groups. But refugee and migrant groups have many features that make separate guidance necessary. Without tailored advice, there is a danger that they will 'miss out' on government initiatives intended to encourage voluntary groups to become service providers, and commissioners will also 'miss out' on the valuable contributions they could make.

---

[4] The difference between grant-aid and commissioning is described in detail in Office of Government Commerce (2004) *Think Smart, Think Voluntary Sector!*, section 4. Practical help for MRCOs in getting established and obtaining grant funding is available from the Refugee Council, Refugee Action, the Migrants' Rights Network and from some of the other organisations listed in appendix 2.

More responsive public services?

Specific guidance has to take account of many special factors – for example, the diverse ways in which groups emerge, and the fact that many are relatively new and may not have infrastructure such as offices or full-time staff. Their experience of bidding for contracts may well be limited and they may be outside the support networks which keep other voluntary sector groups informed of opportunities and policy changes. First generation migrants, lacking experience of British public services, may come from very different cultures where concepts like 'commissioning' or the 'voluntary sector' are unfamiliar and the frameworks and processes are very different.

The guide also aims to take into account the difficult decisions which MRCOs face in considering whether to change their organisations to become formal public service providers. These decisions cannot be taken lightly, and may have implications for the wider role of groups which often act as advocates on behalf of people who struggle to secure the rights and services they deserve. At the same time, not all members of new migrant communities will necessarily *want* services from representatives of the same communities. So decisions about the future role of each MRCO will need careful thought and discussion. The guide is no substitute for that, but it is intended to help the process. The guide makes no value judgement about the decisions made by MRCOs as to whether they become commissioned service providers or not – but chapter 6 aims to help them make those decisions.

Who is the guide for?

The guide has the main aims of *persuading agencies which commission public services* to engage with refugee and migrant groups, and of *helping those groups to consider providing public services* on a formal basis and to 'bid' for contracts to provide those services. Its main audience is the two sides of the commissioning process – agencies across the public sector which commission services that are likely to be relevant to asylum seekers, refugees and new migrants, and MRCOs interested in being commissioned to provide them.

Commissioning bodies – Key parts of the guide

For readers from commissioning bodies who are familiar with the commissioning process, the key parts of the guide are:
- background to MRCOs (chapter 2)
- what they can offer you (chapter 4)
- building their capacity – your role (chapter 7)
- key issues that arise (chapter 8)
- how MRCOs can get started (chapter 9)

It may then be helpful to look at the relevant chapter on your service area in part two.

The guide should also be useful and relevant to second-tier and infrastructure organisations that support the development of MRCOs, including organisations such as the Refugee Council that attempt to influence government policy.

Another audience is the policy and regulatory bodies that influence the commissioning of public services, and have to implement the government's third sector agenda.

Finally, the guide should be valuable in implementing wider government policy towards commissioning and the third sector, because other community-based organisations are often in a similar position to MRCOs and face many of the same issues about the future of their services.

The guide is largely based on research in England, where some MRCOs already have relevant experience, but the principles are relevant to service providers across England, Wales and Scotland (and the specific features of Welsh or Scottish commissioned services are referred to wherever possible). However, because so many MRCOs are London-based, especially those who are commissioned service providers, there is an inevitable London bias.

How was the guide prepared?

Some MRCOs already do deliver commissioned services. Where experience already exists, the guide has tried to learn from it – by discussing with both sides of the commissioning process what went well, what problems occur, what obstacles have to be overcome, and what lessons could be useful for other groups. In the course of preparing the guide, the authors met with some 25 groups and a range of commissioning bodies individually, held a series of six seminars across England, Wales and Scotland, and drew on the prior experience in this field of hact and organisations such as the Refugee Council, Scottish and Welsh Refugee Councils, Refugee Action and Praxis.

The kinds of questions asked were these:
- Do MRCOs really provide value for money and are they able to provide effective links between commissioning bodies and new communities?
- What are the barriers to greater engagement?
- What kind of practical advice is needed to enable MRCOs to expand their role?
- What more can commissioning bodies do to encourage them and build their capacity as service providers?
- What tests will MRCOs have to meet and how do these relate to the policy frameworks in which commissioning bodies operate?

How is the guide organised?

The guide is in two parts. The first addresses the general questions that apply to any group planning to become a service provider, and to any commissioning body planning to engage with MRCOs. The second looks in more detail at the requirements of particular commissioned services, and is aimed at groups which have decided which service areas they want to enter. It will also be of interest to commissioning bodies in those service areas that want to look in more detail at the possibility of commissioning MRCOs, and how those groups may go about 'bidding' to be service providers.

Part one consists of chapters 2-9. Chapter 2 is aimed mainly at commissioning bodies and provides background material on who and what MRCOs are, and what they already do. Chapter 3 is an overview (mainly for MRCOs) of public sector reform and how commissioning fits within it. Chapter 4, aimed at both commissioners and MRCOs, sets out the case for MRCOs being service providers, and how this fits into wider objectives for public services. Chapter 5 then briefly describes the range of services where MRCOs might particularly have a role. Chapter 6 poses the questions that MRCOs need to ask themselves *before* considering whether to become providers of commissioned services. Chapter 7 is about building the capacity of these community-based groups as potential service providers. Chapter 8 deals with some of the common issues that crop up – the opportunities, risks and obstacles – from the viewpoints of both MRCOs and commissioners. Chapter 9 is also aimed at both sides of the commissioning process and is about how they get started in this field.

Part two then has eight separate chapters on the main services which are likely to be commissioned from MRCOs, describing the policy framework and the requirements of the commissioning process in sufficient detail to provide groups with the information they need to enter the field. These chapters do not exhaust all the possibilities for MRCOs to become commissioned service providers, but they do aim to cover the services which provide the main opportunities for them to do so.

Terms used in the guide

For simplicity and clarity, some terms are used in the same way throughout the guide. The first set of terms relates to the commissioning process and is shown opposite.

The term 'procurement' is often used interchangeably in policy documents with the term 'commissioning', but to avoid doubt in the guide only the term 'commissioning' is

Introduction

commissioning	The whole process of assessing need, identifying resources available, planning how to use the resources, arranging service delivery, and the reviewing of service and reassessing of need[5]
commissioning body	An agency responsible for entering into, funding and monitoring contracts for publicly funded services
service providers	Those contracted to provide commissioned services
both 'sides'	In the commissioning process, used as shorthand to refer to the commissioning bodies and service providers, taken together
third sector	The range of organisations, which occupy the space between the state and the private sector – these include small local community and voluntary groups, registered charities both large and small, foundations, trusts and the growing number of social enterprises and co-operatives. Third sector organisations share common characteristics in the social, environmental or cultural objectives they pursue, their independence from government, and the reinvestment of surpluses for those same objectives[6]
social enterprise	A business with primarily social objectives whose surpluses are principally reinvested for that purpose in the business or in the community, rather than being driven by the need to maximise profits for shareholders and owners[7]
service level agreement (SLA)	A formal agreement between a service provider and the body for whom the service is performed (often used to indicate something short of a formal contract)

used except when 'procurement' occurs in source documents. (To be consistent with this, the EU 'procurement rules' which govern public sector commissioning, are called in the guide 'competition rules'.)

Some further terms relating to capacity and capacity building are defined in chapter 7.

The groups and communities to which the guide refers are defined overleaf (these groupings may, and often do, overlap with each other).

---

5 Taken from Local Government Association (2004) *From Vision to Reality – Transforming outcomes for children and families*, p12.
6 Taken from DH (2006) *No Excuses. Embrace Partnership Now! – Report of the third sector commissioning task force* (available at www.dh.gov.uk).
7 Department of Trade and Industry (2002) *Social Enterprise: A Strategy for Success*.

black and minority ethnic (BME)	people, groups or communities that would not be categorised as 'white British' in the census definition (and therefore embracing asylum seekers, refugees and other migrants, as well as long-established BME groups)
refugee community organisation (RCO)	a body led by refugees and acting on behalf of or providing services for refugees and/or asylum seekers
migrant community organisation (MCO)	a similar body led by (mainly non-refugee, but also newly-settled) migrants, such as economic migrants from EU member states and elsewhere
umbrella organisations	bodies – often called forums or councils – which bring together refugee and migrant groups across a local authority area

For more information on the background to and definition of terms relating to refugees and asylum seekers, and the eligibility of new migrants for various services, please refer to other guides such as *Housing and Support Services for Asylum Seekers and Refugees*[8] and to the joint project by hact and the Chartered Institute of Housing, Opening Doors.[9]

---

8   Perry, J (2005) *Housing and Support Services for Asylum Seekers and Refugees – A good practice guide*. Chartered Institute of Housing for the Joseph Rowntree Foundation.
9   See www.cih.org/policy/openingdoors/ and www.hact.org.uk/downloads.asp?PageId=173

PART ONE

Chapter 2

MRCOs – the Background

> **What this chapter is about**
> - characteristics of MRCOs
> - how they are developing
> - how RCOs and MCOs differ
> - government policy towards MRCOs
> - finance for MRCOs
> - the kinds of services they already provide

Who and what are MRCOs?

In chapter 1 we defined 'refugee community organisation' as a body led by refugees and acting on behalf of or providing services for refugees and/or asylum seekers. 'Migrant community organisation' means a similar body led by (mainly non-refugee) migrants, such as economic migrants from EU member states. Both types range from informal groups that are just getting going to long-established ones with full-time staff.

Many MRCOs serve particular national or ethnic groups (Somalis, Kurds, etc). Some cover broader geographical regions (Africa, Latin America), or are culturally based (Arabic, Francophone). Yet others focus strongly on women's needs, deal with particular issues (children, disability, etc) or are focused on professions (eg the group Voice of Britain's Skilled Migrants). MRCOs are found throughout Britain but are especially numerous in London (where there are more than 500 RCOs alone)[10] and also in significant numbers in cities like Birmingham, Glasgow, Cardiff and elsewhere. Some (but very few) are found in smaller towns and rural areas. Overall numbers of MRCOs are not known, but there is a cautious estimate of 'as many as 1,000' RCOs in England[11] and about 25 in Scotland.[12]

---

10 Zetter, R et al (2005) *Refugee Community Organisations in the UK: A social capital analysis* (available at www.esrcsocietytoday.ac.uk).
11 An estimate by the Refugee Council based partly on RCOs known to them.
12 An estimate by the Scottish Refugee Council.

How do MRCOs develop?

MRCOs are typically formed by a small number of committed refugees or migrants who often operate from someone's home or a community centre before gradually acquiring premises and funding. They may start by serving a particular nationality, often by providing basic advice on access to services. Their gatherings enable asylum seekers, refugees and other migrants to come together, share information about their country of origin and discuss issues of concern to them.[13] Many groups have considerable demands made on them by asylum seekers, particularly those whose applications have been refused and who have limited or no resources.

Like any community-based groups, MRCOs represent a spectrum from newly formed organisations (perhaps set up in response to new groups of migrants moving to a particular place, possibly because of asylum dispersal or because of work opportunities) to long-established bodies with a history of serving refugees or migrants over many years. In large cities there may be several MRCOs at various stages of development – the most advanced perhaps already providing services like those discussed in this guide.

There are various stages in the development of MRCOs, although they are not necessarily sequential and not all groups pass through all stages. This is a brief and therefore highly simplified description:[14]

- First is the *emergence* of a new group, perhaps in response to new migration clusters.
- Second is *formalisation* of the group, adopting a constitution and possibly obtaining grant funding for its activities.
- The third stage is *enhancement and specialisation*, in which the group adopts and develops particular roles and enters into formal relationships with public sector and other agencies.
- Finally there is *wider engagement*, for example when the original groups form umbrella bodies (such as city-wide refugee networks or forums), infrastructure (or second-tier) agencies or operate in networks at national level (many of these agencies are mentioned in appendix 2).

There has been significant growth in the numbers of MRCOs, mainly (outside London) in response to dispersal or very recent economic migration. In some larger

---

13 Based on Gameledin-Ashami, M et al (2002) *Refugee Settlement – Can communities cope?* (available at www.ces-vol.org.uk).
14 The complexities of the development of small, community-based groups are illustrated in Kumar, S and Nunan, K (2002) *A Lighter Touch: An evaluation of the governance project.* JRF, which worked with 20 emerging groups, including RCOs.

cities such as Birmingham, there are examples of groups at all of the stages just mentioned and indeed the history would reveal groups which have developed but later disbanded. Many of the migration-related groups are recently established, but others, such as London's East European Advice Centre established in 1984, have experienced massive demands for their services following recent growth in migration.

Another feature of MRCOs is the diversity of aims, and the diverse ways in which different groups see themselves. For example, while all provide services at least at a 'self-help' level, some may see themselves as mainly advocacy groups – challenging immigration decisions or indeed immigration and wider policy. At the other end of the 'spectrum', some groups may be registered as companies, or even be social enterprises – with a strong entrepreneurial drive. Yet others have a mainly cultural or faith focus. And of course some embrace all of these elements.

Another issue of relevance in commissioning is the complex pattern of groups that emerge in some localities: for example, one ethnic or nationality group might have a number of different representative organisations in one area. This happens for various reasons – such as the politics of communities living in exile, because different groups provide different specialist services, or simply because a large country like Somalia is not homogeneous but has different communities within it.

In Scotland, where the growth of MRCOs is related mainly to recent dispersal of asylum seekers, many are now preoccupied by the recent high rate of negative asylum decisions, which is also affecting their leadership and limiting their capacity to develop.

How do RCOs and MCOs differ from each other?

People involved in different kinds of RCO and MCO who attended the seminars held in preparing this guide suggested the following differences as being most important:

- Refugees are often profoundly affected by the trauma associated with forced migration, and this can affect their ability to integrate, whereas other migrants can often 'hit the ground running' and integrate more quickly.
- Communities evolve from being mainly refugee to being mainly migrant communities, and the same applies to their community organisations. Latin Americans, for example, no longer really see themselves as a refugee community.
- Some communities overlap – for example, Somali immigrants from other EU countries are statistically 'migrants' yet may have similar needs to Somali refugees.

- Refugees and other migrants often live in different areas.
- Refugees may have been subject to 'dispersal' but then have moved from dispersal areas once they became accepted refugees.
- RCOs work with asylum seekers and are often not concerned about the legal status of their clients – which may be a factor affecting their ability to tender for commissioned services. Also, they are often supporting people in very vulnerable circumstances, which may be less the case for MCOs.

What is government policy towards the development of MRCOs?

There has been no single policy decision or major funding programme (as there was, say, with black and ethnic minority housing associations) that led to MRCOs being formed over a particular period of time, although Home Office policy has progressively recognised their existence and the roles that they can play. The most recent statement of policy in England is in the government's refugee integration strategy, *Integration Matters*.[15] Despite official encouragement, however, RCOs have been described as occupying an 'ambiguous and precarious position' in contemporary Britain.[16]

> ### Policy towards RCOs in *Integration Matters*
>
> 'The enormously valuable work of RCOs in helping refugees to acclimatise to life in the UK has already been emphasised. Based on the self-help principle, and usually run on slender resources, they build links between refugees and the wider community and provide English-language training and employment support. They also offer expert advice to local, regional and national government on the problems faced by refugees in accessing services, achieving their full potential, and contributing to communities. We want to boost the capacity of RCOs to undertake this, particularly through the carefully targeted use of the government funding available for refugee integration work.'
>
> *Integration Matters*, para 3.15.

In Scotland, the Scottish Government established the Scottish Refugee Integration Forum (SRIF) which published an action plan in 2003, and a progress report on its implementation in 2005.[17] In Wales, the Welsh Assembly Government (WAG) has a

---

15 Home Office (2005).
16 Zetter *et al* (2005). See footnote 10.
17 Available at the Scottish Government website (www.scottishexecutive.gov.uk/Publications/2003/02/16364/18139).

draft refugee inclusion strategy.[18] In both Scotland and Wales, given that their communities and MRCOs are less mature, policy is to develop and strengthen them rather than to promote their role as providers of commissioned services.

As yet there is no policy towards, nor formal recognition of, MCOs, except insofar as they overlap with RCOs or can be identified as BME organisations and therefore benefit from general government policy about BME community groups.

What finance is available to help MRCOs develop?

Limited government funding for RCO development is available through the Refugee Community Development Fund. Some of the other Home Office-administered funds, such as the Challenge Fund, can benefit RCOs. In addition, a number of the proposals made in *Integration Matters* which are still under development are intended to help to promote RCOs in future (for example, planned advice and consultancy services for RCOs).[19] There is limited support for RCOs in Scotland, and in Wales there is a proposal for a funding stream which has not yet been implemented.

Most groups depend however on a combination of locally accessed public funds and/or sources such as grant-making trusts and the Lottery. The various sources are too numerous to describe here.[20] Some RCOs have succeeded in getting 'core funding' (to pay for their central running costs) as well as funding to provide particular services or projects. However, often the funding is temporary whereas needs are permanent (or at least, long-term).

On-going reliance on short-term grants or 'seed corn' funding causes a range of problems:[21]

- uncertainty
- energy devoted to fundraising instead of providing services
- difficulty in building expertise because staff are temporary or insecure
- competition for funding between projects
- pressure to 'innovate' or establish new projects even when there is an established need for an already-existing service.

---

18   Available at the WAG website (http://new.wales.gov.uk/topics/housingandcommunity/consultation/closed/refugeeinclusion/?lang=en).
19   See Home Office (2006) *A New Model for National Refugee Integration Services in England*.
20   A good description of sources of grant funding, and associated problems for RCOs is Tyler, P and Khan, N (2006) *Funding for Refugee and Asylum Related Projects: Availability and Access*. National Consortia Co-ordinating Group (available at www.partnershipdevelopmentproject.org.uk).
21   Perry, J (2005), p99.

One argument for RCOs becoming commissioned service providers is that it is a way for them to secure longer-term stability in their funding while also prioritising services which are needed by the communities they serve.

What kinds of services do MRCOs provide?

A study of 22 London-based RCOs summarised their 'significant contribution' to refugee resettlement as:[22]

- providing cultural and emotional support and opportunities for 'developing identity'
- delivering practical assistance and advice, including interpreting services and addressing problems about access to public services
- raising awareness and understanding (about refugees) in the community
- inputting to policy development.

Outside London, because RCOs have often developed more recently, the proportion making such a 'significant contribution' may be lower, but there are still many that do show these characteristics.

Because the origin of most MRCOs is as 'self-help' groups in some form, experience of providing services at some level is widespread. From such experience, needs for more developed services may be identified, especially if there are local service 'gaps' – or mainstream services exist but they are not oriented to the needs of migrants, lack appropriate language expertise or are otherwise not culturally sensitive. Groups which develop such services may well also gain significant expertise – for example, in culturally sensitive approaches to mental health issues.

MRCOs providing significant services may do so either as wholly non-profit groups or as 'social enterprises' (see chapter 1) whose profits are principally reinvested in the community. This distinction may in practice be imprecise, or groups may be in transition from one stage to another. In many cases, to gain accreditation as service providers, groups will have to clarify their constitutional position (see chapter 9).

MRCOs and Community Cohesion

An important issue about the future funding of and service provision by MRCOs (and indeed BME community organisations generally) has been raised in the report of the

---

[22] Gamaledin-Ashami, M et al (2002) *Refugee Settlement: Can communities cope?* Charities Evaluation Unit and Evelyn Oldfield Unit.

Independent Commission on Integration and Cohesion, the Singh Commission.[23] It has questioned the principle of what it calls 'single group funding' – that is, funding awarded 'on the basis of a particular identity, such as ethnic, religious or cultural'.

The Commission says that there should be a presumption against single group funding unless there is a clear need for capacity building within a group or community. It says that, if single group funding is nevertheless awarded:

- reasons should be publicised to all communities in the local area
- before receiving further funding, the group should demonstrate how it is becoming more 'outward facing' and starting to follow integration and cohesion principles.

The Commission also recommends government to:

- produce guidelines about single group funding that reflect integration and cohesion principles
- ensure that mainstream services (that is, ones that are supposed to be available to everyone) 'improve their offer' to particular communities so that single group funding is no longer felt necessary.

The Commission recognises new arrivals as a need group but does not specifically exempt services to them from its recommendations.

These and other aspects have been challenged by third sector organisations, and the outcome in terms of government policy or guidelines is not yet known. Nevertheless, in the light of the Commission's concerns, the guide suggests that MRCOs and commissioners address the following questions:

- If the service is to meet needs for people who cannot yet be expected to access mainstream services easily, such as new migrants, does it include an element which will help them to access mainstream services in the future (rather than encourage continued dependency on the special service)?
- If the need is for a culturally sensitive service, can the need be specified clearly and the additional requirements compared with a mainstream service made clear?
- Can such a service be delivered in a way that promotes integration, for example by offering the service more widely and to different communities?
- Can the project or service be used to influence mainstream provision or facilitate access to it, for example by helping people with paperwork or by showing mainstream providers what the gaps are in their services?
- Is the organisation providing the service engaged with other communities and can it show how its services contribute to community cohesion more widely?

---

23 *Our Shared Future*, published in June 2007, is available from the Commission's website (www.integrationandcohesion.org.uk) together with supporting documents.

As this guide also demonstrates, the role or potential role of MRCOs is not confined to service provision, but (as the government's third sector policy recognises) includes identifying emerging or 'hidden' communities, ensuring that commissioning bodies better understand different kinds of need, enabling commissioners to engage with communities, and piloting alternative methods of working with 'hard-to-reach' groups.

MRCOs and commissioning bodies will need to keep themselves informed of developments when the government decides policy on this and other issues, based on the Singh Commission's work.

Chapter 3

Commissioning and Public Sector Reform

What this chapter is about
- what the government's different 'agendas' mean
- what commissioning means
- what commissioning bodies are looking for in service providers
- how commissioning relates to the 'efficiency' agenda
- what 'modernisation' of local public services means

What are the 'agendas' for public sector reform?

The different policies which government is pursuing (often called 'agendas') have different names and overlapping purposes. As well as the 'commissioning model' there is also an 'efficiency' agenda, the 'best value' approach to service delivery and the 'modernisation' of local government. These all come under the broad umbrella of 'public sector reform', which places many new pressures on those delivering public services, including:

- providing more choice to the consumer
- commissioning services from different providers, not just from one
- testing the need for services, not just assuming that a need exists
- demonstrating value for money (often involving putting services out to tender)
- setting standards and judging performance according to 'outcomes'
- achieving efficiency savings, so that more can be done with the same resources
- devolving responsibility and making services more accountable to consumers
- creating a stronger role for the third sector in providing services.

In a particular sector, some aspects of the reform agenda may be more developed than in others. For example, where user involvement is being promoted strongly, this may create more opportunities for MRCOs to help shape services and possibly deliver them.

Public sector reform in Scotland and Wales has many similar elements to that in England, but without the same emphasis on commissioning.[24] In Scotland, the equivalent of promoting the third sector is promotion of the 'social economy' – which has a dedicated website with guidance on tendering and other material.[25] The potential contribution of the social economy to public services is reflected in the reports *Transforming Public Services: the next stage of reform*[26] and *Better Value: Purchasing public services from the social economy*.[27] Communities Scotland has also produced specific guidance on securing 'social value' (explained later, in chapter 8).[28]

This chapter aims to provide a guide to what the package of policies called 'public sector reform' means for MRCOs – particularly in the context of their potential role as service providers. For this reason, 'commissioning' is picked out as the most important of the different 'agendas'.

What is commissioning about?

'Commissioning' can be defined as:[29]

> '...the process of specifying, securing and monitoring services to meet individuals' needs at a strategic level. This applies to all services, whether they are provided by the local authority or by the private or voluntary sectors.'

This is a wide definition, and we need to explain it in more detail by putting it into context. Increasingly, public services are moving to a 'commissioning' model, in which they are no longer the direct service provider (or, if they are, not the *only* service provider), and services are commissioned from other bodies, the private sector and the third sector.

---

24   Information is available on the Scottish Government and WAG websites (for Scotland see www.scotland.gov.uk/Publications/2006/06/15110925/0 and for Wales http://new.wales.gov.uk/about/strategy/makingtheconnections/?lang=en).
25   www.socialeconomyscotland.info
26   Scottish Government (2006) (available at www.scotland.gov.uk/Resource/Doc/172410/0048184.pdf).
27   Communities Scotland (2007) (available at www.communitiesscotland.gov.uk/stellent/groups/public/documents/webpages/cs_017271.pdf).
28   Communities Scotland (2006) *Making the Case: Social Added Value Guide* (available at www.communitiesscotland.gov.uk/stellent/groups/public/documents/webpages/otcs_014654.pdf).
29   Taken from Audit Commission (2004) *Making Ends Meet,* an online resource on social services commissioning (downloadable at www.joint-reviews.gov.uk/money/commissioning/2-contents.html).

Commissioning is therefore part of a big 'culture change' affecting all parts of the public sector. Because this change is recent and the whole field of commissioning is still growing, it is not surprising that public sector agencies (as 'commissioning bodies') are often still getting to grips with it, and may not be familiar with every relevant policy development. The pace of change is also different in different sectors.

While commissioning is supposed to be a comprehensive, structured process, in practice commissioning bodies have often had to 'get to grips' with the process of contracting out *first*, and may be still developing or refining their approaches to other aspects such as assessing needs and reviewing performance. Government has also acknowledged that many bodies lack the skills necessary for commissioning.

While commissioning bodies often put considerable effort into devising the policies they apply, they are also subject to other 'top down' pressures from government departments and ministers to meet efficiency targets (see below) or simply to cut budgets. In addition to the culture change just described, many services – notably health – are subject to organisational upheavals which can cut across or disrupt other changes. As one of the groups interviewed for this guide commented: 'commissioning bodies don't set the agenda, it's set above them.'

What are commissioning bodies looking for in service providers?

It is essential that MRCOs who wish to become service providers are familiar with the expectations of commissioning bodies. This section is about the general approaches which commissioning bodies are likely to follow, in the context of government policy towards public services and third sector involvement in them. (Specific requirements of particular programmes are dealt with in part two of the guide.)

Value for money is the main objective

The overriding concern of commissioning bodies is always to achieve value for money in service provision. The government explains value for money (VFM) in this context as follows:[30]

> 'VFM is not the lowest price – it is defined as the optimum combination of whole life costs and quality to meet the user's requirement.'

---

30 Office of Government Commerce (2004) *Think Smart, Think Voluntary Sector!*, p13.

Another way of expressing value for money is by listing the tests which commissioning bodies will apply in purchasing services. These have been summarised as: [31]

> 'buying the services
> - at the right price
> - at the right quality
> - of the right quantity
> - at the right time, and
> - in the right place'.

These requirements can also be summarised as 'the three Es': economy, efficiency and effectiveness. As government commissioning advice emphasises:[32]

> '...don't confuse obtaining value for money with awarding contracts on the basis of lowest initial price.'

In other words, it is not only 'economy' that is important but also 'efficiency' and 'effectiveness'.

The starting point for obtaining VFM is a clear statement of what the service provider wants. This is often called the *service specification* or *user's requirement*, and it includes any specific level of quality or standard of service which the commissioning body expects, and this must be tested critically for need, cost-effectiveness and affordability. In other words, the specification cannot simply be set in a way that favours particular suppliers over others – it has to relate to the needs which the service aims to meet. The specification is most likely to avoid this trap and promote innovation in service provision if it judges performance using 'outcomes' not just 'inputs' or 'outputs' (see box on next page for explanation of these terms).

VFM is central to the public procurement (or competition) rules, based on EU legislation, which control the commissioning process.[33] Achieving VFM usually requires commissioning bodies to put services out to competitive tender.

MRCOs bidding for commissioned contracts must, above all else, be able to make a value-for-money case in relation to their potential competitors. This may not be as difficult as it seems – smaller organisations may have lower overhead costs or other advantages. One local authority commissioning officer speaking at one of the seminars

---

31 Adapted from DTI (2003) *Public Procurement – A toolkit for social enterprise*, p19.
32 Office of Government Commerce (2006) *Social Issues in Purchasing* (available at www.ogc.gov.uk).
33 See the procurement policy guidelines in chapter 22 of *Government Accounting*, available at www.government-accounting.gov.uk, although the full EU rules do not apply to community services such as health, education and social services, where greater flexibility is allowed.

More responsive public services?

Inputs, outputs and outcomes in service specifications

An input specification might say that the contractor has to provide an area office in a particular place, with four staff. But it says nothing about what those staff are expected to achieve. An output specification might say that they have to deal with so many cases per week. But such a quantitative specification says little about the quality of the service. This might be done by specifying measurable outcomes. Some examples are:[34]

- fewer people needing emergency hospital admissions
- fewer people losing their tenancy
- more people finding jobs
- fewer people reporting feelings of isolation and low self-esteem
- fewer people being admitted to long-term residential care.

Outcome specifications often require information to be collected on people's views (eg their level of satisfaction with the service they have received), as well as quantitative data on the results of the service.

The way that costs, inputs, outputs and outcomes relate to VFM and economy, efficiency and effectiveness is summarised in this diagram:

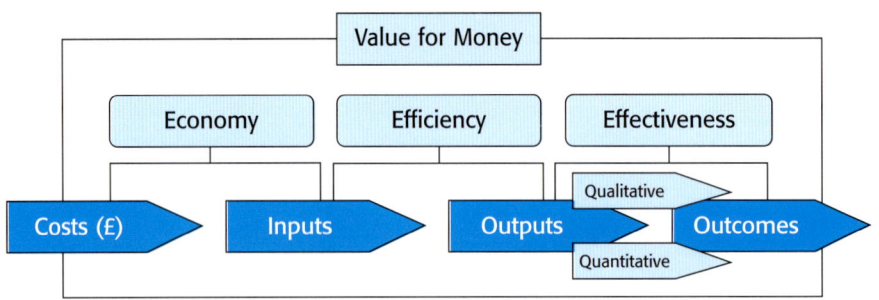

Source of diagram: Audit Commission (2004) *Making Ends Meet*.

held when preparing the guide commented that they had compared overhead costs and found out that, except in one case, those of small organisations were often lower than those of large agencies. This is because most of their income goes directly to the salary of the worker. There are some issues of quality, but other gains (user involvement, community development, etc) more than compensate for this.

---

34 Taken from ODPM (2003) *Assessing Value for Money in Supporting People Services* (available at www.spkweb.org.uk). This is a useful guide to assessing VFM for support services generally.

On the other hand, a recent Audit Commission report[35] quotes the comment that:

'Voluntary organisations often claim that they add value, but are not skilled in explaining what value they add and how they add it. Voluntary organisations will need to develop answers to these questions, because it is unlikely that the public sector and other funders will see things in exactly the same way.'

Promoting competition and 'choice'

Recent government pronouncements[36] have placed a much stronger emphasis on 'choice' in public services. The main approach to providing greater choice is to have a bigger range of service providers, offering different services and in competition with each other. To do this, the government may have to 'develop the market' – create a situation in which customers expect more choice, and more providers then become available.

Market development and supplier diversity

Government guidance makes it clear that the competition rules allow commissioning bodies to help to 'develop the market' by promoting 'supplier diversity' – encouraging a range of different suppliers, from the public, private and third sectors. The argument is that, even if a monopoly supplier might be cheaper in the short term, long-term VFM is more likely to be secured by having a range of suppliers offering choice to the customer, innovative approaches and in competition with each other.

Service user involvement

Another key element is user involvement in service provision, including the commissioning process itself, with funding following the choices which those users make. One advantage of the third sector over (say) the private sector is that it can often demonstrate strong community links and service user involvement, including their involvement in running the organisation itself. The government recognises this, but also that there can be tensions (which we come back to later) between representing service users and actually providing the services.

A role for the third sector

Government has committed itself to achieving a greater role for the third sector in service provision. Making greater use of the third sector is therefore likely to be an important factor in achieving supplier diversity at local level (as well as in creating greater choice and user involvement). But it is the commissioning bodies who effectively determine whether this objective is achieved, across a range of public services, and often they are at local level. The government encourages them to

---

35 Audit Commission (2007) *Hearts and Minds: Commissioning from the Voluntary Sector*, p27.
36 Summarised in NCVO (2005) *Voluntary Sector Strategic Analysis 2005/06*.

endorse its aim and make their commissioning practices 'third sector friendly'. The ways in which this might be done are dealt with in chapter 8.

Within the third sector, government is also committed to promoting the role of BME organisations, which are often less involved in service provision than 'mainstream' voluntary groups, but are of course also likely to be closer to their respective communities. MRCOs can argue that they reflect the needs of sections of the BME community that are often overlooked.

More details on the growing role of the third sector – and particularly BME organisations – as service providers are given in the next chapter.

Achieving wider social and environmental benefits

The extent to which commissioning bodies can use the commissioning process to secure wider benefits for the community or take account of social issues (such as the need for local jobs) is limited by the competition rules. But it does still exist – and it may be extended as greater use is made of Local Area Agreements (see below). The key test is that the wider benefits are directly relevant to, rather than incidental to, the nature of the contract. This can be best demonstrated by including them within the user requirements, as part of the original specification (rather than introducing them at the stage where the contract is awarded). So, for example, requiring service providers to demonstrate how they will tackle social exclusion as part of the contract might be relevant to commissioning a regeneration or renewal service in a neighbourhood where the local authority has a published policy to reduce social exclusion.

More information on specifying wider benefits (and the role of MRCOs in this) is given in chapter 8.

Strengthening civil society

Part of government's interest in promoting the third sector is its desire to strengthen what it calls 'civil society', or the range of bodies that operate at local level, especially community-based ones. It wants these local bodies to have a stronger role in building positive community relationships. Many MRCOs can demonstrate ways in which they contribute to local communities – for example, by bringing together groups from different ethnic backgrounds, or helping people to integrate better into their neighbourhood.

Balancing VFM and other aims

Commissioning bodies have to balance the secondary aims just mentioned (such as supplier diversity, user involvement and achieving wider social benefits) with the *primary aim* of securing value for money. In practice, VFM is an overriding requirement in many cases (however committed the commissioning bodies may be to the other aims), simply because of financial pressures. For example, Supporting

People funding is being cut in real terms at the same time as demand for services is increasing (and MRCOs may themselves identify new needs – see chapter 8). Similar pressures exist in most other service areas.

Commissioning and the 'efficiency' agenda

The drive to greater efficiency in delivery of all government programmes[37] is another source of pressure on commissioning bodies. It is leading them to look for service providers who can offer economies of scale and take on more of the risk associated with funding programmes (eg the risk of overspending towards the end of the financial year). It is important that MRCOs who want to become service providers are also familiar with the 'efficiency' agenda and can show how they can help a commissioning body to address it. At the same time, they also need to bear in mind the risks of underpricing their services – which we discuss in chapter 9. A summary of the efficiency agenda is given in the box.

The government's efficiency agenda – a brief summary

Efficiency is 'the best use of the resources available for the provision of public services'. There are four ways to achieve efficiency:

reducing inputs	increasing outputs
reduce inputs for the same outputs (eg same level of service, fewer staff)	more outputs or better quality from the same inputs (eg work to higher standard within the same budget)
reduced prices (eg of procurement) for the same output (eg pay the provider less, but service level stays the same)	proportionately more outputs or better quality with proportionately less increase in resources (a better result than spending extra money on an alternative)

Quality can be defined in various ways:
- *technical* – measuring outputs against a defined standard or specification
- *customer* – meeting customer needs, eg responsiveness, reliability, accessibility of the service
- *value for money* – where quality and cost combine to produce a service which meets technical and customer requirements at an acceptable level of expenditure.

Source: CIH and HouseMark (2006) *Integrating Quality and Efficiency* (www.cih.org).

---

37 Instigated in England by the Gershon report – see Gershon, P (2004) *Releasing Resources to the Front Line*. HM Treasury. In Scotland, the Scottish Government published the Efficient Government Plan in 2004 (see www.scotland.gov.uk/Publications/2004/11/20318/47372).

Commissioning bodies want to work with suppliers who can help them to meet their efficiency targets, in one of the four ways set out in the box. MRCOs can use this agenda to their advantage. For example, although one way of achieving efficiency is to cut costs (which might favour large suppliers), another is to achieve better outcomes for the same inputs – and MRCOs are well-placed to provide more culturally sensitive services than large suppliers and engage with 'hard-to-reach' groups within the community.

Commissioning and the 'modernisation' agenda for local government

The government also has a broader 'modernisation' agenda for local public services which cannot be described in detail here.[38] Its aims fit within the overall drive for public sector reform just outlined. For example, it expects local authorities to become more 'strategic' bodies on behalf of the local community, commissioning services from the rest of the public sector, the private sector and the third sector, without in all cases being service providers themselves. But there are other specific aspects of the modernisation agenda for local government that will affect the role of MRCOs (details below cover England, and are followed by a note on Scotland and Wales):

Local Strategic Partnerships (LSPs)

Local Strategic Partnerships are overall bodies created to bring together the three sectors (public, private, third) to set a 'strategic vision' for the local authority area, lead the drive to improve public services and address the government's wider 'sustainable communities' agenda. As well as their overall role, they also include 'thematic partnerships' on issues such as crime prevention, improving the health of the community, and so on. LSPs also have a specific role in promoting the 'commissioning model' at local level.

As part of the third sector, BME groups may be involved in LSPs, but so far there is very little involvement of newer migrant or refugee groups.[39] However, some LSPs have focused on issues directly relevant to such groups, such as refugee integration or community cohesion strategies. MRCOs may be able to become involved in LSPs or thematic partnerships through umbrella organisations.

---

38 See the local government white paper: CLG (2006) *Strong and Prosperous Communities* (available at www.communities.gov.uk) for proposals for local government reform in England. In Scotland, many reforms were included in the Local Government in Scotland Act 2003.

39 Low levels of involvement by BME communities in LSPs are criticised in the report by the Black Training and Enterprise Group (2007) *Participation and Local Strategic Partnerships*, CRE (available at www.equalityhumanrights.com/pages/eocdrccre.aspx).

Local Area Agreements (LAAs)
One aspect of the modernisation agenda which the government is now promoting more strongly is the concept of Local Area Agreements.[40] Under these, agencies come together to agree priorities and share budgets in order to address particular 'cross-cutting' issues. Some LAAs have adopted themes particularly relevant to MRCOs – for example, Leicester's *Community Cohesion – Learning to Live Together*.

But the LAA 'agenda' is widening and as it does so it will provide more opportunities, particularly for community-based groups. LAAs are seen in the local government white paper[41] as having a much bigger role. In future, local authorities will have to prepare a single LAA, and other bodies such as PCTs, the LSC and the JCP will have to be partners in it and agree to the targets (based on 'outcomes') which it contains. Third sector organisations and local communities will have to be consulted in the development of the LAA, although there has been criticism of limited involvement by the third sector in LAAs so far.[42] One limitation of the LAA is that each relates to a single authority area – producing complications for MRCOs in cities like London whose work crosses boundaries between authorities.

Many sources of government funding to local services will in future be directed through the LAA instead of through separate funding streams, and the LAA will be the mechanism for deciding how the funds are allocated. It is therefore vital that MRCOs keep up-to-date with the detail of LAAs as they develop.

Empowering communities
This is another important – but so far not clearly defined – aspect of local government modernisation. The idea is to empower communities by giving them a bigger role in shaping service delivery or even in delivering services themselves. Neighbourhood-level management of services will be promoted, and 'devolution' of service delivery can take different forms – for example, tenants running their own estates. The government intends to issue guidance to authorities on how this will affect commissioning:[43]

> 'This will place citizens and users at the heart of service commissioning and will emphasise the need to involve the public in the design of local services, especially those who might otherwise be marginalised. We will also identify best practice in extending choice and involving citizens and users throughout the commissioning cycle.'

---

40   For general material on LAAs, see the pages on the CLG website (www.communities.gov.uk/localgovernment/performanceframeworkpartnerships/).
41   CLG (2006) *Strong and Prosperous Communities*, chapter 5.
42   National Audit Office (2007) *Local Area Agreements and the Third Sector: Public Service Delivery* (available at www.nao.org.uk).
43   CLG (2006), p32.

Part of the devolution of services can involve community-based bodies (such as MRCOs) in the third sector in actually running services. But the extent to which this develops will depend on local initiative (and pressure from local third sector organisations), as well as being subject to the competition rules mentioned earlier. One good example is Haringey (see page 81 and 96) which sees its role as not just commissioning services but taking a strategic interest in developing local groups in what is a multi-ethnic borough.

Better procurement

All local authorities are supposed to be modernising their approach to procurement (of goods and services they use directly, such as construction or ICT), and there is a joint strategy for procurement between the government and the Local Government Association.[44] This sets targets for local authorities to achieve in improving their processes, one of which is having a strategy which shows 'how the council will encourage a diverse and competitive supply market, including small firms, social enterprises, ethnic minority businesses and voluntary and community sector suppliers'.

The DTI's Social Enterprise Unit has provided support for a network of local authorities focused on finding *New Approaches to Public Procurement*.[45] The NAPP network is helping local authorities to implement procurement pilots (including social enterprises – see next chapter) which maximise training and job opportunities for disadvantaged residents. One of these is in Sheffield.

Sheffield's Community Enterprise Development Unit

Sheffield Council is one of the 'NAPP' authorities and specifically aims to promote enterprises that will employ local people in deprived communities. It has a dedicated development unit (www.scedu.org.uk) to assist new social businesses.

Achieving 'best value'

There is also an overriding commitment that public bodies should secure 'best value' in service provision, defined as delivering 'the quality of service that people expect at a

---

44   ODPM (2003) *National Procurement Strategy for Local Government in England (2003-2006)*. For procurement guidance in Scotland, including the *Review of Public Procurement in Scotland – Report and Recommendations* (2006), see the Scottish Government website (www.scotland.gov.uk/Topics/Government/Procurement).
45 The *New Approaches to Public Procurement* network of local authorities (NAPP) works to address the obstacles to achieving wider social benefits through public contracts (contact them on 0121 200 3242). The Social Enterprise Unit has now become the Social Enterprise and Finance Team in the OTS.

price they are willing to pay'.[46] This means that services should be commissioned from outside bodies where there is a best value (or value for money, a similar concept) case to do so. Best value (BV) is based on the 'four Cs' of consultation, comparison, competition and challenge.

Many public services undertake BV reviews of their effectiveness, which need to involve service users. The local government white paper places less emphasis on BV, but does say that BV means that services should 'involve the citizen as the shaper of services'.[47] MRCOs are well-placed to consult service users in their communities, and even make BV comparisons across an area through their umbrella organisations.

The performance framework
All public service providers have some kind of regulatory or inspection regime. Local authority performance is assessed by the Audit Commission. Authorities are currently subject to a Comprehensive Performance Assessment (CPA) and given an annual rating between 'excellent' and 'poor'. In making its overall assessments, and assessments of individual services, the Audit Commission uses various key lines of enquiry (called 'KLOEs') as well as data from best value performance indicators (BVPIs).[48]

Particular KLOEs may be relevant to MRCOs. For example, there is a housing KLOE (number 31) which specifically addresses 'diversity' and asks questions such as whether there are links with BME communities to ensure that services are tailored to their needs.

The performance framework for local government is also changing to reflect the desire for public sector reform.[49] Although it is going to be streamlined and detailed elements will change, the new version will still emphasise efficiency, the commissioning model and involvement of service users.

Local government in Scotland and Wales
In Scotland, policy towards local government has several elements in common with those just described, in particular best value. Performance is assessed by the Audit Scotland on a three-yearly basis. Community planning in Scotland is roughly the equivalent of LSPs mentioned above, but is longer-established and based on the 32 local authority areas.

---

46   Quoted from Garnett, D and Perry, J (2005) *Housing Finance*. Chartered Institute of Housing.
47   CLG (2006), p114.
48   CPAs are described on the Audit Commission website (www.audit-commission.gov.uk/cpa/index.asp).
49   CLG (2006), chapter 6. CPAs will soon be replaced by Comprehensive Area Assessments – see details on the Audit Commission website, above.

In Wales, the equivalent mechanism to the LSP is the community strategy, prepared by all 22 local authorities. Best value has been replaced by the Wales Programme for Improvement[50] which is similar to CPAs in England, and local government performance is assessed by the Wales Audit Office.

How is local government responding to public sector reform?

Local government's response to all these reforms is likely to result in major changes in its approach to working with the third sector. These are only now beginning to take place, and will work through more quickly in some places (eg large local authorities) than others.[51] The changes will represent both opportunities and threats to MRCOs.

One example is the policy change by London Councils (formerly the Association of London Government), which distributes £28m of funding annually to the third sector on behalf of London boroughs. It has moved away from grant funding towards commissioning specific services – including services for refugees.[52] Instead of groups asking for funding to help them deliver whatever happens to be their speciality service, London Councils will 'decide on priorities and the services that should be funded, and then look for the groups best able to deliver them'.

One good practice point that has been adopted is to consult widely on the service specifications, encouraging community-based organisations to comment on them. London Councils worked with a second-tier organisation (the Evelyn Oldfield Unit – see appendix 2) to help empower the organisations to respond effectively.

Another stance on commissioning and the changing local government role was taken by a local authority commissioner who attended one of the seminars connected with the work on the guide. He said:

> 'Local authorities shouldn't see themselves as just procurers of services, but should enable communities to run services for themselves.'

While the changes described may be a threat to the funding of some groups, they also potentially provide opportunities for MRCOs that did not exist before. These opportunities are discussed in the next chapter.

---

50   See the Wales Audit Office website (www.wao.gov.uk/whatwedo/426.asp).
51   An assessment of progress in achieving the third sector 'agenda' for local government has been made by the Audit Commission (2007) in *Hearts and Minds: Commissioning from the Voluntary Sector* (www.audit-commission.gov.uk).
52   These plans take effect from 2007/08 and it is essential that MRCOs interested in being commissioned to provide services to London boroughs are familiar with them (for latest details see www.londoncouncils.gov.uk/cat.asp?cat=2258).

Chapter 4

What MRCOs can offer to Commissioning Bodies

What this chapter is about
- the range of advantages MRCOs can offer
- the role of MRCOs in delivering better services
- the role of MRCOs as part of the 'third sector'
- other reasons for the use of MRCOs as service providers

What are the reasons for commissioning MRCOs as service providers?

Chapter 3 summarised the government's approaches to reforming the public sector, and suggested some of the opportunities for (and threats to) MRCOs. This chapter aims to help both commissioning bodies and MRCOs understand the contribution that MRCOs can make in helping to deliver better services and achieve these wider government objectives. It also aims to help MRCOs develop in detail their case for being service providers, against this background.

The 'case for MRCOs' is made under three headings:

- that MRCOs can help to deliver better services
- that MRCOs are an important part of the 'third sector' with which commissioning bodies now have to engage
- that there are other policy and legal reasons why commissioners should engage with MRCOs.

An important point to make at the outset is that the potential role of MRCOs is not necessarily obvious to commissioning bodies: they need to be *convinced* (and, as we said in chapter 1, this is one important reason for having this guide). In addition to the pressures and targets described in the last chapter, commissioning bodies are usually under acute time constraints, and their ability to look for new ways to deliver services (including 'nurturing' the third sector) may be limited in practice even if they have policies which say that they will do so. Their limitations may be as much to do with their own staff shortages or limited expertise, as it is to do with the inexperience of many third sector organisations in competing to provide services. So, even if commissioning bodies are not blind to the advantages of working with MRCOs, they may simply not have the resources to do so.

Many of the wider aims for the public services described in chapter 3 are very recent and their impact is being felt differently in different services. MRCOs therefore have to be *very clear* that they can provide at least the same value for money as mainstream service providers. They need to argue convincingly that their role is not only compatible with the policy aims as they apply in each service, but *positively helps to bring them about.*

How can MRCOs help to meet the objectives of delivering better services?

Government guidance on developing the role of the third sector in providing services suggests a range of advantages that the sector can offer in service delivery, compared with public and private sector service providers. The headings in the box below are adapted from this guidance[53] and are used to set out the actual or potential advantages that apply specifically to MRCOs as service providers (as part of the wider third sector). The text also quotes from a speech by Ed Miliband,[54] the previous Minister for the Third Sector.

Comments under each heading are informed by the interviews with MRCOs carried out for the guide.

> ### What can MRCOs offer as service providers?
>
> *Specialist knowledge, experience or skills*
> MRCOs have knowledge of the needs of asylum seekers, refugees and new migrants, based on their own shared experiences. They understand how to deliver culturally sensitive services to these groups, including having skills in relevant languages that would be expensive for other providers to develop themselves.
>
> →

---

[53] See Office of Government Commerce (2004) *Think Smart, Think Voluntary Sector!*, section 5, and HM Treasury (2002) *The Role of the Voluntary and Community Sector in Service Delivery – A cross-cutting review*, section 3.
[54] Available at www.ncvo-vol.org.uk/press/speeches/?id=3621

They have specialist knowledge directly appropriate to service provision (eg knowledge of local solicitors and their strengths/weaknesses in dealing with immigration problems). Many studies have shown that refugees and other migrants have high education and skill levels that may be under-used because of language issues or lack of opportunities.

Ability to involve people in service delivery
MRCOs have experience of using and encouraging volunteers, both from within their 'own' community and (for example) from faith groups. They may be less bureaucratic than mainstream providers (eg in catering for volunteers, paying expenses, etc). Their committees or boards include service users or people from the same community. Or as Ed Miliband put it, they have the 'ability to engage and empower and reach out'.

Independence from existing and past structures and patterns of service
Adopting – often out of necessity – a 'holistic' approach to people's needs comes naturally to MRCOs, rather than attempting to channel people into particular services. They can act as a link to mainstream services for people who would otherwise be marginalised or left out, as well as filling gaps in mainstream services.

Access to the wider community without 'institutional baggage'
While not necessarily 'representative' in a formal sense, MRCOs often maintain a range of formal and informal contacts within their community that is richer than would be possible for other providers. MRCOs have an important role as advocates for their communities, or as Miliband said 'the capacity to be a voice for the voiceless'.

Freedom and flexibility from institutional pressures
MRCOs are able to offer responsive services not driven by public sector budgets and targets or private sector emphasis on the 'bottom line'. They can provide a relaxed, trusting environment and can have an instinctive understanding of clients' problems because of their own experiences.

Ability and willingness to innovate
MRCOs may be less risk averse and more strongly motivated than other potential service providers, and therefore more able to experiment and adopt new approaches. They have (as Miliband said) the 'ability to innovate and think about social problems anew'.

Responsiveness to service users' needs
MRCOs may be highly focused on particular services or sectors of the community and therefore more alert and responsive to change. They may be much more accessible than mainstream providers, providing a more welcoming environment to people who may be nervous about accessing services. As one interviewee for this guide commented: 'MRCOs can deliver quality because they are passionate about what they do'.

→

Ability to operate in 'niche markets'
Niche markets are available to MRCOs that are too small or specialised to be attractive to bigger providers. They can serve client groups that would remain 'hidden' to mainstream providers, including people from other marginalised groups who come to them because they are local, trusted and culturally sensitive in what they do.

Can help the commissioning body to build its capacity
Commissioners often know little about the needs of refugee and migrant groups. MRCOs can help them fill their knowledge gap and extend their skills. In a situation where commissioners need to find out about new demands arising from migration, but where there is little official information available, MRCOs can provide both qualitative and quantitative advice in establishing levels of need.

Economies of scale
While MRCOs do not have the size to offer economies of scale, where they are specialists in a particular field, they can offer efficiencies in other forms (see box on page 37) that would be difficult for bigger, non-specialist providers. As one group commented: 'big is not always best'.

These comments are of course general and may not apply in particular cases. And what for some organisations may be strengths could be weaknesses in others – they could be too responsive and not selective in what they do, or they could be so close to the community that they do not inspire trust on sensitive issues.

Equally, experienced MRCOs may have even more to offer than was suggested above. Some already have experience as service providers, as is clear from the examples in this guide. In some cases they have developed innovative management and administrative systems to equip them to relate to different commissioning bodies with different accounting and monitoring requirements. Some MRCOs may want to build on their experience of operating in one service area, by expanding into others.

Commissioning bodies can use the range of advantages sketched out in the box as a starting point for exploring the actual skills and experience of local MRCOs. Similarly, MRCOs can use the list as the basis for their own, more detailed 'organisational *curriculum vitae*' which shows more fully what they are able to offer.[55]

---

55 Communities Scotland has published (2006) *Making the Case: Social Added Value Guide* (www.communitiesscotland.gov.uk/stellent/groups/public/documents/webpages/cs_013301.hcsp) which provides tools to enable organisations to demonstrate the added value they can provide.

What is the 'third sector' agenda?

The government's third sector agenda, mentioned in the previous chapter, has several aspects relevant to the role of MRCOs, including:

- advocating greater user involvement in services – with the third sector having greater possibilities to ensure this through volunteer involvement and community contacts
- looking for more diversity in service provision – moving some sectors (like the health service) away from being solely public sector providers, towards becoming commissioners – and the third sector's involvement is part of this
- reaching poorer communities and 'hard-to-reach' groups
- providing services in ways which are more sensitive to user needs and offer greater choice.

As we have said, this agenda is being driven from the top – by the Cabinet Office's Minister for the Third Sector and by the Treasury – and is being followed with varying levels of enthusiasm by different departments. For example, while the Department of Health has a special task force to push for more commissioning from the third sector, the Home Office's recent paper on refugee support services[56] does not mention the sector.

Although bodies like the National Council for Voluntary Organisations (NCVO) support the government's policy, there are also important issues and questions – for example:[57]

- is the commitment to the third sector genuine, or is it being used to deflect criticism from private sector involvement in services like health?
- or is it really about saving money?
- will it be mainly big third sector organisations that benefit, or will it reach down to smaller bodies (like MRCOs)?
- can the change lead to real *transformation* of public services, not just *transferring* the service from one provider to another?
- on the other hand, will it lead to third sector bodies giving up their role of challenging government?

The third sector agenda can create opportunities to radically change services, putting the user first, avoiding gaps between services, offering real choice and producing better outcomes for the same money – as well as reaching out to everyone in a community and tackling social exclusion. But it is important that pressure is maintained on government and on commissioning bodies to ensure that this really happens.

---

56   Home Office (2006) *A New Model for National Refugee Integration Services in England.*
57   Based partly on Blackmore, A (2006) *How Voluntary and Community Organisations can help Transform Public Services* (available at www.ncvo-vol.org.uk).

The government now has an action plan for third sector commissioning which sets out eight principles (see box) that are supposed to be applied by commissioners.

> ### The government's principles for commissioning and the third sector
>
> The government believes that all commissioners of services should:
> - develop an understanding of the needs of users and communities by ensuring that, alongside other consultees, they engage with third sector organisations as advocates to access their specialist knowledge;
> - consult potential provider organisations, including those from the third sector and local experts, well in advance of commissioning new services, working with them to set priority outcomes for that service;
> - put outcomes for users at the heart of the strategic planning process;
> - map the fullest practicable range of providers with a view to understanding the contribution they could make to delivering those outcomes;
> - consider investing in the capacity of the provider base, particularly those working with 'hard-to-reach' groups;
> - ensure contracting processes are transparent and fair, facilitating the involvement of the broadest range of suppliers, including considering sub-contracting and consortia-building where appropriate;
> - seek to ensure long-term contracts and risk sharing wherever appropriate as ways of achieving efficiency and effectiveness; and
> - seek feedback from service users, communities and providers in order to review the effectiveness of the commissioning process in meeting local needs.
>
> Source: Cabinet Office (2006) *Partnership in Public Services: An action plan for third sector involvement*, p18.

The action plan goes on to promise that government will reduce the barriers to third sector involvement by steps such as having standard contracts, funding over a period of years (rather than short term), allowing full cost recovery (see chapter 9), facilitating subcontracts and consortia (see chapter 8), promoting the use of social clauses in contracts (see chapter 8) and developing the third sector's capacity (see chapter 7).

The government has published a wider review of the role of the third sector, showing in details how it is taking the agenda forward. The interim report[58] referred to the work needed to ensure that smaller organisations can become service providers, as well as

---

58   HM Treasury (2006) *The Future Role of the Third Sector in Social and Economic Regeneration: Interim Report* (available at www.hm-treasury.gov.uk).

larger ones. The full review[59] has a range of measures or proposals relevant to small third sector providers, for example:

- a promise of 'continued dialogue' with groups working with BME and faith communities, and with marginalised communities, and that the measures in the third sector review will be 'as accessible as possible to a range of organisations' (section 2 of the review)
- a small grants programme aimed at such groups (section 3)
- better guidance to funders and commissioners on advance payments, long-term funding and risk sharing (section 4)
- an Innovation Exchange, to develop and spread innovative practice (section 4).

Most importantly, the review extends for a further two years the National Programme for Third Sector Commissioning to train commissioners from the main public services, run by the Improvement and Development Agency (IDeA) in conjunction with the Office of the Third Sector.

The government has also reiterated its commitment to closer working with the third sector originally made in the 'Compact' issued in 1998. The Compact was aimed at 'creating a new approach to partnership between government and the voluntary and community sector'. It is described in the box (below).

The government's 'Compact' with the third sector

The Compact is 'a general framework and an enabling mechanism to enhance the relationship between government and the third sector'. Following its publication, detailed 'codes of good practice' were produced on funding, consultation and policy appraisal, volunteering, and black and minority ethnic and community groups.

There was a commitment by government to encourage local authorities to 'adopt and adapt' the Compact to suit their relationship with the voluntary and community sector. Most have now done so – all local authorities in Wales and in Scotland (where the equivalent is a 'voluntary sector policy statement' or 'partnership') have Compacts, and almost all authorities in England. Local health bodies and learning and skills councils have been encouraged to develop Compacts and some have done so. Some of these bodies positively encourage community-based bodies to engage in service provision.

→

---

[59] HM Treasury (2007) *The Future Role of the Third Sector in Social and Economic Regeneration: Final Report* (available at www.hm-treasury.gov.uk).

> In 2006, the government created the Commission for the Compact, responsible for its implementation. In the final report of the third sector review, the Commissioner is charged with carrying out a review of the Compact and its codes, with the aim of having revised documentation in place by early 2008/09.
>
> More information: www.thecompact.org.uk

In Scotland, the Scottish Government has a strategy (*A Vision for the Voluntary Sector – The next phase of our relationship*) and there is a Scottish version of the Compact, also with local Compacts. In Wales, there is an overall Voluntary Sector Scheme, reviewed annually, and local Compacts.[60]

How do MRCOs relate to the third sector agenda?

How do these developments help MRCOs? The eight principles for commissioning (see above) provide useful points that MRCOs can use in making the case to be service providers. The review of the role of the third sector has further measures to include small organisations like MRCOs and some of the capacity-building measures (see chapter 7) may also help.

However, much depends on the ability of the Minister for the Third Sector, using the results of the review, to influence the detail of commissioning decisions which are now made by hundreds of national and local bodies. The difficulty is illustrated by the fact that while nearly all local authorities have local Compacts in place, they are often reported as not being effective in ensuring a role for smaller third sector bodies (like MRCOs) when commissioning of services actually takes place.[61]

What other 'carrots and sticks' exist to encourage commissioning bodies to engage with MRCOs?

The government has a range of other ways in which (at least, in theory) it encourages its own departments, publicly funded agencies and local authorities to engage with bodies like MRCOs and encourage their role as service providers. It does this through:

---

60   See the respective websites (www.scotland.gov.uk/Topics/People/15300/partnership-working/Scottish-Compact and http://new.wales.gov.uk/topics/housingandcommunity/voluntarysector/publications/volschemereport0405?lang=en).
61   A report for London Councils (2007) *Common Themes on Commissioning the VCS in Selected Local Authorities in Greater London* (available at www.londoncouncils.gov.uk/doc.asp?doc=20082) points to the weaknesses in commissioning processes and the pitfalls for BME organisations.

- the commitment to closer working with BME groups generally
- the promotion of 'social enterprises'
- the Home Office's refugee integration strategy
- the CLG's community cohesion strategy
- race equality legislation.

These are described briefly below.

The government also uses the directions and regulatory regime (the 'carrots and sticks') that apply to particular programmes (eg Supporting People). These will be considered in part two where the guide describes individual service areas.

Government's commitment to closer working with BME groups

As part of the wider Compact with the third sector (see above), the government adopted a BME code of practice[62] in 2001, intended to give specific emphasis to the role of BME organisations. It calls for greater consultation with BME groups, and specifically mentions groups representing refugees and asylum seekers. It points out the role which BME organisations have in 'filling the gaps in services' to BME communities, and even in delivering wider mainstream services. It is therefore a useful starting point for arguing the case for greater involvement by MRCOs.

However, evaluation of the code has shown that so far its effect has been very limited. Many BME groups are unaware of it and many public bodies do not push it actively.[63] Calls have been made for a fundamental review of its operation and of the commissioning of services from the BME sector.[64]

In Scotland, the Scottish Government granted core funding for the establishment of the Black and Ethnic Minority Infrastructure in Scotland (BEMIS). BEMIS aims to strengthen the capacity of the black and ethnic minority voluntary sector, raise its profile and at national level, coordinate the voice of the sector and ensure that issues of concern are raised with the relevant bodies (see www.bemis.org.uk).

In Wales, AWEMA (All Wales Ethnic Minority Association – www.awema.org.uk) has funding from WAG to produce a good practice guide and promote the development of BME organisations.

---

62   Home Office (2001) *Black and Minority Ethnic Voluntary and Community Organisations – A code of good practice.* Available at www.thecompact.org.uk
63   Syed, A et al (2002) *Black and Minority Ethnic Organisations' Experience of Local Compacts.* JRF Findings 122. JRF.
64   See the online newsletter *Compact Quarterly*, winter 2006 edition, www.thecompact.org.uk

Promotion of social enterprises

Within its general approach of encouraging third sector bodies to provide services, the government is particularly keen on 'social enterprises' – businesses with primarily social objectives whose surpluses are principally reinvested for that purpose in the business or in the community, rather than being driven by the need to maximise profits for shareholders and owners.[65] It has published a 'toolkit'[66] to help social enterprises become public service suppliers, and it encourages local authorities to promote the role of social enterprises at local level (see box below).[67]

Another recent development is the legal provision to create (or convert other bodies into) 'community interest companies' that use their assets for the benefit of the community. There is general information on this particular form of social enterprise at www.socialenterprise.org.uk/Page.aspx?SP=1626 and detailed guidance is available from the new regulatory body (www.cicregulator.gov.uk).

Among MRCOs, some social enterprises have already emerged, and have won contracts – some examples are included among those in part two. At present, it cannot be said that there is a rigid distinction between non-profit MRCOs and social enterprises: while the majority of MRCOs are quite definitely non-profit, some are moving towards a social enterprise approach.

Cheshire's social enterprise toolkit

The County Council's toolkit is an online resource with detailed information on how to create a social enterprise. It is available from www.cheshire.gov.uk/wellbeing/toolkit/intro.htm and describes how to set up an enterprise in nine stages.

Government strategy for refugee integration

The strategy set out in the Home Office policy paper *Integration Matters*[68] refers to the role of RCOs (but not MCOs) and how the government wants them to contribute

---

65 Department of Trade and Industry (2002) *Social Enterprise: A Strategy for Success*.
66 Available from the Department for Business, Enterprise and Regulatory Reform (www.berr.gov.uk/index.html).
67 More information and case study examples are available from the Social Enterprise Coalition website (www.socialenterprise.org.uk), in Scotland from the Social Economy website (www.socialeconomyscotland.info/content/) and in Wales the WAG website (new.wales.gov.uk/topics/housingandcommunity/regeneration/socialenterprise/?lang=en) which includes the report by WAG (2005) *Social Enterprise Strategy for Wales*.
68 Home Office (2005).

to refugee integration. It says (p36) that government wants to boost the capacity of RCOs, and it recognises the importance of the services they provide for refugee communities. It refers to the significance of certain services for refugees (eg Supporting People, ESOL courses) although without actually spelling out the potential role of RCOs in providing them. It promises that the Home Office will 'work with government departments to fully assess how refugee issues are dealt with and reflected within departmental strategies' (p71), and makes a similar promise about improving links with local government, social services, etc.

RCOs may find it useful to refer to the strategy in arguing for a greater role as service providers, and some may be in a position to tender to provide refugee integration services as these are rolled out nationally in 2008.

Unfortunately, as yet there is no equivalent strategy for the integration of new migrants more generally, and hence for the MCOs that represent them. MCOs therefore have to rely on the more general policies towards BME and other third sector groups.

Community cohesion policy

Government responsibility for community cohesion policy in England moved in 2006 from the Home Office to the CLG, and the second annual progress report on it has been issued.[69] The strategy does not especially promote the role of BME groups as service providers, but does place emphasis on working in partnership with them to reduce discrimination and improve cohesion. MRCOs could usefully stress their actual or potential role in contributing to community cohesion.

The Independent Commission on Integration and Cohesion, which reported in 2007, is proposing a new definition of community cohesion and a wide range of other policy changes. It stressed the importance of taking account of refugee and migrant communities in service provision, and called for community cohesion to be a mainstream issue for public authorities with a new national target.[70] It also raised the issue of what it called 'single group funding', which was discussed in chapter 2 (see page 27).

There is no direct equivalent to community cohesion policy in Scotland and Wales: it is dealt with under the heading of equality policy.

---

69   CLG (2007) *Improving Opportunity, Strengthening Society: Two years on* (available at www.communities.gov.uk).
70   Commission on Integration and Cohesion (2007) *Our Shared Future* (available at www.integrationandcohesion.org.uk).

Equality legislation and policy

The Race Relations (Amendment) Act 2000 placed a general duty on public bodies throughout the UK to promote equality of opportunity and good race relations, as well as specific duties to carry out ethnic monitoring of their workforces, assess the impact of their services on race equality and prepare 'race equality schemes' which show how they are implementing these responsibilities. These requirements do, of course, apply equally to their relationships with new BME communities as they do to long-established ones. MRCOs can refer to the legislation and the race equality schemes published by commissioning bodies, to challenge them to show that they are meeting the needs of new groups such as migrants and refugees (see chapter 9).

Equality legislation is likely to be overhauled following the government's Equalities Review and the establishment of the Equality and Human Rights Commission (EHRC).[71] This is likely to see issues about discrimination and equal opportunities in relation to race and faith brought within the same framework as other equality issues, such as disability and gender. MRCOs will therefore have to make the case for the role they can play in relation to this wider agenda, not only in relation to race, faith, cultural or language issues.

Race equality – legal requirements

Public bodies must have 'due regard' to how they will:
- eliminate unlawful racial discrimination
- promote equal opportunities
- promote good relations between people from different racial groups.

Race Relations (Amendment) Act 2000[72]

The West Midlands Forum – race equality

In 1998, six local councils in the West Midlands set up a forum to develop a common standard for assessing providers on their compliance with race equality legislation. The criteria are included in contract conditions and, once contracts are awarded, the councils monitor contractors to check that they are putting their policies into practice.

→

---

[71] The EHRC website is www.equalityhumanrights.com and the Equalities Review is at archive.cabinetoffice.gov.uk/equalitiesreview

[72] For more detail on diversity issues in procurement, see CRE (2007) *Supplier Diversity: A guide for purchasing organisations* (available at http://83.137.212.42/sitearchive/cre/publs/index.html).

> Under the common standard, providers are asked to send in their written policy on race equality in employment or their general equal opportunities policy. The standard consists of three levels, corresponding to firms of different sizes.
>
> Providers who meet the common standard do not need further race equality checks when they bid for contracts over the next three years.
>
> Further information: www.birmingham.gov.uk

MRCOs also have obligations under equality legislation, which may increase if they deliver public services. These are dealt with in chapter 9.

CHAPTER 5

COMMISSIONED SERVICES THAT MRCOS MAY PROVIDE

What this chapter is about
- types of services provided
- brief descriptions of each one
- signposting part two of the guide

What kinds of services?

Chapter 2 noted that the main types of service likely to be relevant to asylum seekers, refugees and migrants, and therefore of interest to MRCOs as potential service providers, are these:

- accommodation and related services – providing accommodation and giving advice on accommodation issues
- services meeting immediate wider needs – such as interpreting, accessing schools and health services, legal advice, etc
- services meeting people's longer-term needs – providing training and helping people find work
- services meeting community-related needs.

This chapter briefly describes each type of service and (where appropriate) which commissioning bodies operate in that service area. Fuller details on those service areas which provide examples of commissioning are then given in part two.

There is a wider list of opportunities for the third sector in commissioned public services in the government's *Action Plan for Third Sector Involvement*.[73]

---

73   Cabinet Office (2006), chapter 3.

Accommodation and related services

The guide is concerned with those commissioned to provide or manage accommodation on behalf of others, or give advice to people on how to get accommodation. (Some RCOs have become owners of accommodation – as registered housing associations. But very few organisations have achieved this status, and the guide only covers commissioned service providers.)

The commissioning body may be a government agency such as the Borders and Immigration Agency (BIA – which now has the functions originally managed by NASS) or a local authority which wants the service but does not have the accommodation (so the provider's job is to find it as well as manage it). Contracted services include:

- *'Dispersed' accommodation for asylum seekers* – as a contractor or sub-contractor to BIA.
- *'Specialist' accommodation for asylum seekers* – as a contractor to BIA (eg to provide 'hard case' accommodation under s4 of the Immigration and Asylum Act 1999) or to a local authority (eg for unaccompanied asylum-seeking children).
- *Accommodation-related advice or support services* – often provided along with the accommodation itself.

Chapter 10 covers all accommodation-related commissioning.

Services meeting immediate wider needs

These services meet clients' wider day-to-day needs – interpreting, helping with access to necessary services such as GPs and schools, legal (immigration-related) advice, etc.

Commissioned services of this type include:

- *'Induction' services for newly accepted refugees* – the main example of a short-term, general 'induction' service is the Home Office's Sunrise programme, currently being piloted in parts of England and Scotland and due to be rolled out more widely in 2008.
- *Housing-related support* – normally provided under the Supporting People programme, this is a wide category of usually medium-term support services which may be contracted out to MRCOs (see chapter 12).
- *Facilitating access to health services* – providing non-medical support, information, counselling, advice and interpretation, to secure improved access to and use of health facilities for migrant groups (see chapter 13).
- *Legal advice* – provision of legal advice services of various kinds (see chapter 14).

One service under this heading – providing interpretation/translation services – does not yet (to the best of hact's knowledge) provide examples of commissioning. It has not therefore been included in the detailed chapters in part two.

Services meeting longer-term needs

- *Support services for young people* – Connexions is a government-funded service in England which provides wide-ranging support for young people aged 13-19, and MRCOs could be contracted to provide its personal adviser services to young people from migrant groups (see chapter 15).
- *Language training* – ESOL – provided by the Learning and Skills Council (in England) and other agencies (see chapter 16).
- *Employment-related training* – providing job-linked training to refugees, other migrants (and possibly the wider population), usually under contract to Jobcentre Plus (see chapter 17).

Services meeting community-related needs

Although MRCOs are likely to be active in meeting community-related needs, hact is not aware of any commissioned services under this heading, so it is not covered in part two of the guide.

Chapter 6

Providing Commissioned Services – Is it the Right Decision?

What this chapter is about:
- deciding whether to become a service provider
- basic questions that MRCOs need to ask themselves
- carrying out a self-appraisal
- strategic questions about commissioning
- opportunities and threats

Is bidding to provide commissioned services a good idea?

Becoming part of the 'contract culture' will suit some organisations and not others. Many MRCOs provide services, but it is a very big step to become a provider of commissioned services, and it cannot be taken lightly.

This chapter is about the kind of organisational appraisal an MRCO should carry out before deciding to bid to provide commissioned services.

Many MRCOs – even those who provide commissioned services – have reservations about the demands it makes. Comments made by groups interviewed for this guide include the following:

> *'It's like turning into a private sector organisation – but without the salaries that should go with it.'*

> *'Big organisations get the funding to provide services then look to MRCOs to help them deliver.'*

> *'Full cost recovery is no more than what the private sector does – but they get a profit as well!'*

> *'Why should MRCOs provide (commissioned) services? What's in it for them?'*

But also, one MRCO was clear that:

'You have to bid for commissioned contracts if you want to survive.'

What basic questions do MRCOs need to ask themselves?

The majority of MRCOs contacted in preparing this guide expressed interest in providing commissioned services (where they were not already doing so). But some of them were wary of the implications of this model of service delivery on their links with their communities. This is especially true where services are commissioned by agencies with immigration responsibilities – the closer link with the agency might affect the confidence that the community has in their MRCO, or might endanger its role as an advocate for the community. Many MRCOs' work started with helping asylum seekers whose cases have been rejected, undocumented migrants or people with 'no recourse to public funds'. They will want to consider how this work might be affected by moving towards being commissioned service providers.

So the first step is for the MRCO to examine itself and the environment it works in. It needs to reappraise its strengths, weaknesses and what are often called its 'unique selling points' as well as the risks, threats and opportunities which commissioning offers or poses. This is a vital step for an MRCO, even if it then decides *not* to go down the path of providing commissioned services.

How can MRCOs carry out this self-appraisal?

Shifting from providing grant-funded services to delivering commissioned services is a strategic decision which will have a far-reaching impact on the MRCO. Like all other providers, an MRCO will need to carefully assess the feasibility of this move, its possible areas of specialism, and the likely impact, not only on its services but on the whole organisation – its mission, governance structure, accounting systems, personnel, fund-raising, operations, public relations, and facilities and buildings. A leading MRCO involved in commissioning warns other MRCOs that it requires a 'completely different mind set'.

There are different ways of carrying out this kind of self-appraisal. Here we describe two: SWOT analysis and the Hedgehog concept. Whichever is used (or indeed if the MRCO uses another method), the self-appraisal needs careful planning – allow time for it to be done (eg an 'awayday'), get all the key people involved (the board, staff and perhaps some clients or community representatives), and consider using an outside facilitator to ensure that everyone gets a fair chance to 'have their say'.

SWOT analysis

The MRCO needing to take stock of its whole situation and the environment it works in might well use the well-known technique called 'SWOT analysis'. This means looking at

Providing commissioned services – is it the right decision?

the MRCO's strengths and weaknesses, and the opportunities and threats in its operating environment. There are several useful online resources, aimed at voluntary sector bodies, to help in carrying out a SWOT analysis.[74]

The results of a SWOT analysis around the question of whether to follow the 'commissioning' route, might look something like that shown on page 62.

Hedgehog concept

Another useful diagnostic tool is Jim Collins' 'Hedgehog concept' (after the ancient Greek parable 'The fox knows many things, but the hedgehog knows one great thing'.) In this kind of self-appraisal, an organization asks itself the following three questions (quotes below are from the Jim Collins website):

1. *What are we deeply passionate about?* – understand what the organisation stands for and why it exists:
    'The idea here is not to stimulate passion but to discover what makes you passionate.'
2. *What are our unique selling points?* – understand what the organisation can uniquely contribute to the people it touches and to service provision, 'better than any other organisation on the planet'. Equally important, what can you NOT be the best at – and should give up?
3. *What drives our resource engine?* – understand what best drives your resource engine, in three parts: time, money and 'brand'.

The MRCO then needs to consider the intersection of these three circles (see below).

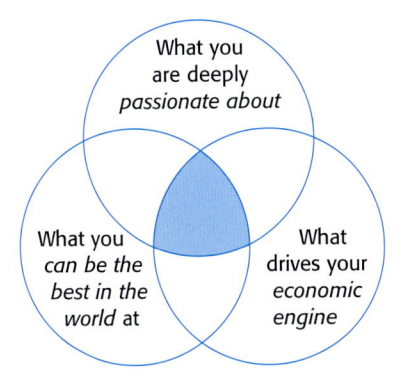

What you are deeply passionate about

What you can be the best in the world at

What drives your economic engine

'What your organisation is deeply passionate about, what it can be best at, and what drives its resource engine – identifying all these helps the organisation to make a conscious and collective choice and reach better understanding of its particular situation and the environment in which it operates.'

---

74 For example: www.voluntarymatters1and2.org/organisation/strategic_planning/more_depth/swot_analysis.html

TYPICAL SWOT ANALYSIS FOR AN MRCO	
OUR ORGANISATION	**RESPONSES**
STRENGTHS • Long-established MRCO with good reputation with official bodies • Good partnership arrangements with other MRCOs • Etc, etc	*How can we MAXIMISE the benefit of these?* • Establish more formal relationship with official bodies eg through commissioning • Examine potential for consortia to deliver services jointly • Etc, etc
WEAKNESSES • Revenue shortfalls forecast for next financial year • Limited capacity to plan beyond one year due to annual funding arrangements • Etc, etc	*How can we MINIMISE or REDUCE these?* • Assess alternative funding sources and whether commissioning would provide more reliable income • Aim for three-year funding streams; consider commissioning opportunities that would provide these • Etc, etc
OPPORTUNITIES • New migrant populations moving into area that have similar service needs to the existing community we serve • Service provider with which MRCO has an established relationship is to start to provide commissioned services • Etc, etc	*How can we CAPITALISE upon these?* • Make contact with new migrant groups to establish scale of community, emerging needs, etc • Seek subcontracting arrangement with them • Etc, etc
THREATS • Loss of service quality as revenue reduces • Other MRCOs offering similar services • There are community tensions in the areas where we work because of population change • Etc, etc	*How can we COUNTER these?* • Continue to drive down costs; diversify income • Consider partnering arrangements to defuse competition and present unified front to public authorities • Examine the possibility of working with wider communities to improve cohesion in the area and encourage contact between different groups • Etc, etc

In addition to better focus and clarity of purpose, the MRCO will also develop the discipline to adhere to and attract and channel resources as far as possible to the intersection of their three circles, and to shun opportunities that fall outside them. It can of course adapt the process as it wishes – for example, the third circle might be 'what are the services which commissioning bodies are seeking to commission or *should* commission?'.

While we did not interview an MRCO that has worked through this particular tool, there are a number that have implicitly known these lessons and have put them to good use. Most organisations that manage to deliver commissioned services successfully seem to have invested in assessing their potential and understanding how the Hedgehog concept applied to them.

Further information on the Hedgehog concept is available at:

www.jimcollins.com/lab/hedgehog/p2.html

Listen to how to find your organisation's three circles at:

www.jimcollins.com/audio/hedgehogA2c.mp3

Strategic questions about commissioning

As part of this appraisal, whichever method is used, part of the time should be devoted to looking at the actual impact commissioning might have on the organisation. Here are some of the 'strategic issues' that need to be faced:

- Does the organisation want to grow? – if so, is this the right direction?
- What mission does the organisation have? – does it want this to change?
- Where does it want to be in 3-5 years' time? – is being a service provider the best way to get there?
- What is the right mix between being a service provider and being an advocate or pressure group on behalf of refugee or migrant communities?
- What are the tensions between these roles and how will they be addressed?
- Can the two roles be successfully combined? – will the organisation be seen as being 'in bed with' the government?
- Are the opportunities to become service providers in the right field, given the organisation's experience and the needs of the community it serves?
- Is there a gap in available services that only this organisation can fill?

- Is the board willing to make the changes and get the new skills it will need if the organisation provides commissioned services?
- Does the organisation have the skills and resources to gear up to being a service provider?
- What happens if time and energy is put into following the commissioning route (eg preparing and making a bid), and it all fails?

As well as these big issues, some smaller ones will immediately come up as soon as a decision in principle has been taken:

- Can the organisation produce documented evidence of its track record in delivering services to client groups, eg casework history and reports to its board?
- What training and development needs are there?
- How will this change affect the current staff? – what expertise is lacking?
- What about the risks? – will the new business actually be viable if the organisation wins it?
- What about cashflow?
- What timetable applies? – is there time to make a proper bid?
- Are there opportunities to learn from other organisations which have gone through a similar process?
- Would it be best to collaborate with other groups through subcontracting or consortia (see chapter 9)?
- Or is entering into commissioned services likely to mean competing with other MRCOs? Is this a problem?

These are all questions that need to be discussed by an MRCO before it commits itself to the time-consuming process of competing to provide commissioned services.

Opportunities and risks in providing commissioned services

It may also be helpful to analyse the opportunities and the risks (or threats) from taking on the role of supplying commissioned services. The box opposite shows such an analysis (based on the case study interviews). Each organisation needs to make its own assessment, however. Part of the self-appraisal exercise just described could include a brainstorming session on the 'pros' and 'cons' of commissioning, then the facilitator could check the results against this list and discuss any differences.

Possible advantages and disadvantages to MRCOs of providing commissioned services	
Advantages	Disadvantages
strengthened financial base	greater financial risk
move away from grant dependency	dominated by need to comply with contract
embracing the 'contract culture'	voluntary ethos threatened
becoming more competitive; making new partnerships	entering a competitive market, including against other MRCOs
secure income over a period	'non-profit' status no longer self-evident
better able to provide key service(s) to client groups	narrower focus - less ability to respond to new or more complex needs
better infrastructure (ICT, etc)	heavy investment required
stronger relationships with statutory bodies	possible loss of advocacy role
sharing information and experience	creates problems for maintaining client confidentiality
ability to develop particular services in a structured way with dedicated resources	pressure to ensure there are clients for the service, possibly at the cost of addressing other needs
better defined services	less flexibility to respond to client needs and provide 'bespoke' services
growth of the organisation	management capacity stretched
formalised policies, eg health and safety	conditions for bidding may be onerous and difficult to meet
incentives to deliver a better, more professional service	greater regulation – by commissioning body as well as by the Charity Commission/Companies House
organisation's status and area of work is properly recognised	have to be sure that the organisation can meet the new expectations placed on it

The Charity Commission has carried out a study of the experiences of charities providing commissioned public services, and as a result has issued new guidance about the legal and good practice issues, to help charities to avoid breaking charity rules or risking their charity status.[75]

A survey by BASSAC[76] has shown that there are longer-term and more profound risks to the character of MRCOs if they become service providers, and of which they should be well aware.

BASSAC's survey of the risks of becoming service providers

In 2005 BASSAC surveyed its member organisations about the shift to a 'contract culture' over the previous three years. Of the 55 members interviewed, 58 per cent said funders had reduced the number of grants for community-led activities. Of these, 56 per cent had seen grants replaced by commissions, contracts and service level agreements.

Some 73 per cent of the groups said that the new systems were making them less secure and 50 per cent said their independence had been compromised. Instead of devising local solutions to local problems, community-based organisations were being forced to compete for contracts to deliver centrally devised programmes.

BASSAC chief executive Ben Hughes said:

> 'The move away from grant funding is reducing the types of work that community organisations are able to carry out and instead they are increasingly becoming service delivery agents designed to fulfil the government's target-driven priorities.'

Although this guide is aimed at helping MRCOs become service providers, the risks to the character of organisations and their community development and campaigning roles should not be ignored. *They may well lead to a decision by an organisation not to take this path.*

---

75 Both the research and the guidance are downloadable (www.charitycommission.gov.uk/supportingcharities/psdindex.asp).
76 www.bassac.org.uk/press.builder/00027.html An academic study of international experiences of third sector organisations and the 'contract culture' is also available (www.icnl.org/JOURNAL/vol1iss4/melville.htm).

Checklist for action by the MRCO's board

✓ have we made the kind of overall appraisal of the direction of the organisation recommended in this chapter?

✓ is the board committed to the new direction the organisation might take?

✓ what are the views of staff? – and service users?

✓ what new business opportunities are available and are they the right ones for the organisation?

✓ have the right contacts been made with the people and commissioning bodies involved?

✓ who else can the organisation learn from?

✓ what are the implications of putting resources into making bids?

✓ do we have the skills and knowledge to start to provide commissioned services?

✓ what change in culture is needed, and how will it be achieved?

✓ what is a reasonable timetable, given the organisation's resources?

✓ how will progress be monitored and problems addressed?

CHAPTER 7

BUILDING MRCO CAPACITY TO DELIVER COMMISSIONED SERVICES

What this chapter is about
- why capacity building is important
- how MRCOs can appraise their capacity
- areas in which MRCO capacity may need building
- ways in which they can build their capacity
- help available to support capacity building
- role of commissioning bodies
- quality assurance systems

Why is capacity building important?

If MRCOs take on contracts to provide commissioned services, without having sufficiently developed their capacity to do so, they are setting themselves up to fail. Being aware of what capacities the organisation has, and even more important what it lacks, is therefore crucial. The guide's starting point is to assume that MRCOs will need to consider their organisation's capacity as part of making their choices about whether to bid for commissioned services, and if so which ones.

This section of the guide is *not* about building the organisation's capacity generally. This means that issues such as obtaining grant funding, agreeing a constitution, or registering as a charity – though important – are not part of the guide. (MRCOs which need such start-up support should approach generic development agencies such as Refugee Action, the Refugee Council, MODA or their local council of voluntary services – such agencies are included in the list in appendix 2.)

This chapter is specifically about the *extra* capacity that established MRCOs will need if they want to move from being grant-funded bodies to delivering commissioned services. But the guide also suggests that MRCOs should look at their capacity *before* making any decisions about commissioning – assessing capacity is part of the decision-making process on whether to go down the commissioning route in the first place.

Although capacity building must spring from action by the MRCO itself, it may be supported by government agencies, capacity-building programmes, infrastructure organisations or in other ways. Commissioning bodies themselves may want to encourage the third sector to act as service providers. As well as the challenge for MRCOs as potential providers of commissioned services, there is also the challenge for these other organisations to identify and work on the specific capacity needs of MRCOs in the new environment. It was clear from discussions for the guide that very few have yet done so, and this chapter should help commissioning bodies who wish to engage with MRCOs in this way.

The chapter starts by looking at the areas relating to commissioned services in which MRCOs may need to develop their capacity. It then considers how they can do this – ways of carrying out the capacity-building process, outside sources of help, and the related issue of quality assurance (or how you demonstrate that you have the capacity, once you have developed it). Finally, the chapter suggests alternative models of engagement in contracted service provision which some MRCOs might use as a stepping stone towards commissioning.

Capacity building has some jargon of its own: there is a glossary of the main terms used in the box below.

	Capacity building – key terms
capacity	the resources available to an MRCO (including people, money, equipment, expertise and information) - especially those relating to its ability to act as a provider of commissioned services
capacity building	activities aimed at increasing the capacity of MRCOs - including training, advice and use of specialist expertise
governance	an organisation's board (or organising committee); how they are selected and what skills they need; the responsibilities they have, and the way they decide the organisation's strategy and ensure that it is carried out (see page 71 for a more formal government definition) →

strategy	the organisation's goals for the next few years and the broad means for achieving them – reflected in its budget, and often in a 'business plan' or other strategic document[77]
infrastructure	the physical facilities, structures, systems, relationships, people, knowledge and skills that exist to support and develop, coordinate, represent and promote frontline organisations, thus enabling them to deliver their missions more effectively[78]
infrastructure organisations	organisations that support service providers, often with special skills or knowledge (eg of migrant and refugee services); also known as second-tier organisations
quality assurance	the range of ways in which an organisation can implement quality management through use of a formal system to encourage improvements

How might MRCOs need to build their capacity?

There are now many publications or web-based resources intended to help voluntary organisations to build their capacity. The potential 'gaps' that organisations like MRCOs might need to fill are often set out under the following six headings:[79]

- governance
- developing an effective workforce
- improving performance
- financial management
- developing ICT resources
- recruiting and developing volunteers.

We have judged these possible 'gaps' based on the interviews undertaken for the guide. Of course, particular MRCOs may have only some of these needs, or none at all, and each MRCO will need to make its own assessment of its 'gaps'.

---

77 Examples of 'strategic issues' faced by MRCOs as potential service providers are given at the beginning of chapter 9.
78 From the ChangeUp website (www.changeup.org.uk/overview/jargon.asp).
79 For example, in Home Office (2004) *Change Up – Capacity Building and Infrastructure Framework for the Voluntary and Community Sector*. Available (with other useful resources) from the Office of the Third Sector website (www.cabinetoffice.gov.uk/third_sector/).

Governance

Governance is 'the systems and processes concerned with ensuring the overall direction, effectiveness, supervision and accountability of an organisation'.[80] MRCOs are often established by a small group or in some cases by dedicated individuals. Sometimes this leads to the so-called 'founder syndrome' where it becomes difficult to differentiate between the organisation and its founding member. Also, because refugee communities are often highly politicised, some MRCOs might become a contested platform for various rival groups.

Governance issues which MRCOs may need to tackle include:
- Lack of awareness or understanding of what 'good governance' requires, including the respective roles of board members and staff.
- Recognising the importance of regular 'audits' of the skills available on the board of the MRCO.
- Developing board member skills to a higher level (commensurate with becoming a service provider, eg addressing the government's 'efficiency' agenda – see chapter 3).
- Recognising the value of recruiting or co-opting board members with skills that are missing in the current board, possibly from outside the MRCO's own community.
- Reluctance of board members to take on extra personal responsibility (eg their financial liability as trustees of a more complex organisation).
- Ensuring the right balance between setting the strategy of the organisation and paying sufficient attention to detail.
- Poor understanding of staff needs – such as training and support – perhaps because the board has a strong volunteer ethos.
- Shortage of good support material to develop the capacity of boards, and possible unwillingness of commissioning bodies to finance it.
- Having mechanisms for dealing with conflicts (including conflicts of interest) where boards and staff are members of the same community or even the same family.

Developing an effective workforce

Workforce development issues that MRCOs may need to tackle include:
- Recognising the importance of investing in the development of the paid and voluntary workforce.

---

80 See reference in footnote 79, p33.

- Unwillingness of funders to finance the cost of staff development.
- Placing too much emphasis on traditional formal training, rather than on modern methods including peer group learning, coaching, shadowing and mentoring.
- Training providers not always understanding the culture and context of the sector or the skills that people working and volunteering for frontline organisations need.
- Recognising the diversity of the community it serves, and ensuring that this is reflected in the workforce.
- Being able to show that it complies with equality law, and take on the greater responsibility that will apply if it provides commissioned services.
- Possibly having to shift the organisation's focus from being oriented to one ethnic minority community, towards services being open to all.
- Attitudes having to change from 'grant dependency' to 'service provider' – in which continued performance and providing value for money to the commissioning body will determine the future.
- Embedding the efficiency agenda and a culture of service improvement in the organisation.

Improving performance

Performance improvement issues that MRCOs may need to tackle include:

- Changing from short-term funding cycles which have forced organisations to be opportunistic, towards a more strategic approach as service providers.
- Commissioning bodies' possible unwillingness to pay for the costs of performance improvement.
- Adapting to quality requirements imposed by commissioning bodies and regulators – even when there is uncertainty of the difference they will make to outcomes for service users (see chapter 3).
- Learning how to 'gear up' to the performance levels expected by commissioning bodies.
- Adopting quality assurance measures.
- Keeping up to date with rapidly changing policy developments affecting commissioning, and changes in rules/requirements that affect bids and contracts.

Financial management

Financial management issues that MRCOs may need to tackle include:

- Being able to demonstrate a sufficient level of financial management to satisfy the requirements of commissioning bodies.
- Adapting to and complying with commissioning bodies' monitoring systems.
- Understanding how to price their services, make bids and secure 'full cost recovery' (see chapter 9).
- Learning how to manage risk (eg sudden fall in demand for services, or policy changes that affect demand) and how to decide what risks there are and who carries them (especially in subcontracts or consortia).
- Managing more complex cash flows (possibly after having relied on regular grant payments).

Developing ICT resources

ICT (information and communications technology) issues that MRCOs may need to tackle include:

- Lack of strategic understanding of how ICT can benefit frontline organisations.
- Difficulties in accessing advice, information and support that is affordable, reliable and relevant to the sector.
- Lack of understanding of the full costs of ICT with a corresponding reluctance by funders to meet those costs.

AdvicePro

Developed by Advice UK and the Law Centres Federation, AdvicePro, available from summer 2007, provides comprehensive casework software for independent advice centres and law centres. The system provides an online case management system with the ability to retrieve and analyse data and meet the latest requirements of funders and regulators – such as the Legal Services Commission.

The system is web-based; it can be accessed by office, home and outreach workers and permits whole case transfer between organisations for referral purposes.

Further information: www.advicepro.org.uk

Recruiting and developing volunteers

Volunteer issues that MRCOs may need to tackle include:

- Developing a proper policy about the use of volunteers (possibly using resources of local volunteer bureaux, etc).
- Continuing ability to recruit, train and manage volunteers, in the new context of the MRCO being a (paid) service provider.
- Maintaining service continuity if the service relies partly on volunteers.
- Helping people to adapt to a highly regulated culture (eg health and safety, child protection, financial accountability, confidentiality, etc), particularly as commissioned service providers.
- Understanding different roles (eg a volunteer may be both a service provider for, and a board member of, the MRCO).

One World Foundation Africa develops its volunteer resources

OWFA (see example on page 152) was funded by the Russell Commission to develop a strategy for involving young BME volunteers in its programmes. As part of this process, OWFA carried out a series of consultations with local area organisations and young people, both volunteers and non-volunteers, to explore their attitudes and experiences of volunteers and volunteering. The consultation report (May 2006) and accompanying strategy document offer a good starting point for organisations wishing to involve young people in their volunteering programmes or improve their volunteering experience for young people.

Further information is available from http://archive.cabinetoffice.gov.uk/russellcommission/report/index.html and from the 'v' website (www.wearev.com).

Resources on volunteering from the Evelyn Oldfield Project

The Evelyn Oldfield Project has various resources available:

- a publication *Working with Volunteers: A Management guide for refugee community organisations* (available at www.evelynoldfield.co.uk/publications/volunteer_handbook.pdf)
- a Volunteering Development Project, running across London, open to refugee-led community organisations which want to improve their use of volunteers
- other resources available from their website www.evelynoldfield.co.uk

Other possible gaps

The list above is by no means exhaustive, and there may well be other areas where MRCOs need to strengthen their capacity in relation to commissioning, that will be apparent from reading this guide. For example:

- It may be necessary to demonstrate the need for a service which does not already exist, and make the case for funding (see chapter 9). This will require skills in collecting objective and reliable data and using the information to persuade the commissioning body to change its priorities.
- Commissioning bodies may want to see evidence of the MRCO's commitment to community cohesion objectives (see page 109), and it may not yet have explored this area of work.
- Similarly, MRCOs may claim to involve service users and to be closer to the communities they serve, but can they demonstrate this? How involved are service users in running the organisation and how does the MRCO learn from the feedback it gets?
- Some organisations may have no (or only an informal) business plan and will need to be able not only to develop one but have the ongoing capacity to ensure it is implemented.
- Organisations may have no experience of bidding for contracts and, in addition to the financial issues mentioned, may need tender-writing skills.
- One aspect mentioned in discussions for this guide was 'resilience to change' – the MRCO's ability to adapt to and cope with a changing environment, including the challenges described in this guide.

Each MRCO will have to tackle its capacity-building needs against the goals which it has for its own development as a service provider. The rest of this chapter is about ways of doing that.

How can MRCOs build their capacity?

Government-assisted and other programmes for capacity building are dealt with in the next section. Here the guide considers the steps which any MRCO might follow in deciding whether and how to improve their capacity. The guide cannot give detailed advice on what can be a complex process – but it does aim to point MRCOs in the right direction.

The assumption is that the MRCO has carried out the kind of overall appraisal (through a technique such as SWOT or the Hedgehog concept) that was discussed in chapter 6. It should then be in a position to look more specifically at its capacity 'gaps' and how to fill them. There are various ways to do this, apart from using outside advisers (which will be dealt with in detail next). For example:

Learning from other MRCOs

An excellent way for small organisations to build their capacity is by learning from similar bodies that have already done so. This may be done in a variety of ways – including visits, exchanges, 'mentoring' or 'shadowing' for key staff, co-opting board members with skills from other bodies, and secondments or recruitment of staff with skills from elsewhere. Hact has encouraged links between emerging RCOs and established ones from the same community (eg an Iranian group in London assisting one in Newcastle). The disadvantage is that it takes time – which many MRCOs do not have.

Recruiting staff with relevant skills

One of the MRCOs interviewed for this study had successfully recruited two key members of staff who had experience of working in relevant parts of the public sector, and they brought this expertise with them to the MRCO. One had particular experience in commissioning. The MRCO has now diversified into several different service fields.

Private sector help on a voluntary basis

Private sector companies (eg lawyers – see example on page 81) may be willing to second staff to an MRCO to build capacity in a particular area of work. Again, there may be an element of mutual benefit, with the secondee also learning about a different customer group.

These may be insufficient, however, and the MRCO may need to seek specialist help – for example, support from an infrastructure (or second-tier) organisation, or hiring a consultant. The rest of this section considers ways of doing this.

Obtaining specialist help

As we are considering MRCOs that want to become commissioned service providers, we can assume that at the outset they will already have some of the basic organisational capacities, and will be in a position to consider carefully what they want to get out of the capacity-building process, and some idea of what weaknesses they need to address. If they aim to develop their capacity for a specific purpose, eg to be in a position to subcontract to a commissioned service provider, then this objective may guide the review or health check.

Using a consultant

If using outside help such as a consultant or infrastructure organisation, they may want to prepare a brief for the exercise which reflects their specific needs (not simply accept a standard review developed for a variety of circumstances). One possibility is that the MRCO asks for or is offered capacity-building help by a commissioning body (see chapter 8). In this case it should have given some consideration to its ambitions for commissioning and what position it wants to be in as a service provider after (say) a period of five years (for example, as part of the SWOT or Hedgehog concept exercises discussed earlier).

Ideally, the MRCO will look for an overall capacity check that identifies all the gaps, and then enables it to prioritise those that need to be dealt with most urgently in the context of moving towards commissioning. Outside organisations or consultants typically start by looking at big issues such as an organisation's goals and its strategies for meeting them, in addition to the detailed matters covered earlier in this chapter. Here is an example.

Consultancy support from the Evelyn Oldfield Unit

The Evelyn Oldfield Unit supports individual refugee organisations through consultancies. Although help is usually requested around one aspect of the organisation, the support is designed to look comprehensively at all areas of management and service delivery. Consultancy support is time-limited and confidential, aiming to have clear outcomes.

A contractual agreement is made between the unit, the organisation and the consultant, and an ongoing relationship is maintained throughout. Members of the organisation's management committee and key staff are expected to participate actively in the work. A holistic approach is used, examining operations, finance, governance, managing people and how these parts work together.

At the start of a consultancy, a member of staff from the Unit visits the group and carries out an in-depth analysis of the organisation's needs based on current difficulties, the culture, structure, social role, purpose, internal and external influences. A plan of action is drawn up and a consultant is found with the right skills to carry out the agreed brief.

Further information: www.evelynoldfield.co.uk

Assessing gaps in the MRCO's capacity

Different experts and 'toolkits' are available for carrying out capacity checks, and they will approach the task in different ways. Typically the stages in the process include:

- *Agreeing the brief* – If an outside consultant is being used, it makes sense to agree the brief jointly, to take advantage of their experience. It will be useful to agree at the outset whether the consultant is also to be engaged to do the follow-up work to help fill the gaps identified.

- *Agreeing the approach* – Different experts or toolkits use different methods, but basic issues are bound to be the degree of access which the consultant has to people and materials in doing the work, and the timeframe to be followed. Assuming that a trusting relationship exists, it is best to be as open as possible. For example, it is vital to involve the MRCO's chair and possibly other board members, key staff, some frontline staff and some volunteers. In a small organisation, this may involve everyone.

- *Designing the capacity check* – This involves deciding the key capacities that are needed and reducing them to a manageable set of questions that will reveal whether they exist. The aim is not to cover every single facet of an organisation's operations, but to pose questions which will identify all the important weaknesses. The questions asked therefore need to reflect the purpose of the exercise (eg to prepare the MRCO to become a commissioned service provider).

> **Example questions for a capacity check on financial management**
>
> As an example to illustrate what the toolkit does, the part that looks at (say) financial management might pose a series of questions which in themselves are about detail but which build up a picture of the organisation's strengths and weaknesses in that area. Some of them may be:
>
> - is there a board member with financial experience and skills?
> - is there a manual of financial procedures available to all staff, setting out responsibilities?
> - is someone responsible for checking that goods or services have been received before an invoice is paid?
> - is a cash flow forecast prepared on a regular basis (say every six months)?
> - is there a way of ensuring that the source of funding for all items of expenditure can be identified, if the organisation has multiple funding sources?

- *Carrying out the capacity check* – The questions might be put to key board members and staff by the consultant, or they might be asked to fill in a questionnaire relevant to their responsibilities, or there may be a group discussion (or some combination of these). The questions are usually answered in standard ways, eg a choice between 'always', 'normally', 'sometimes' or 'never', to provide manageable results.

- *Making the 'diagnosis'* – The results enable a score to be built up for each aspect of the organisation's capacity. The consultant uses this to identify and report back on overall strengths and weaknesses, gaps that are critical to the purpose of the exercise (eg not having records that enable equal opportunities issues to be monitored) and other gaps in skills, procedures or other areas of capacity that need to be addressed.

- *Agreeing the result* – The MRCO will not want to blindly accept the diagnosis, but will want to probe the results and agree what the critical areas for action are, especially in the context of its timetable for becoming a service provider.

Filling the gaps

In many cases the consultant carrying out the capacity check will also have the skills needed to work with the MRCO to fill the gaps. Whether or not it is done with outside help, an action plan needs to be drawn up, with responsibilities allocated, and a timetable and appropriate resources to carry it through. There need to be arrangements for monitoring progress against targets in the plan, to ensure that it is followed through.

Typical actions included in the plan might be:

- having an event such as an 'awayday' to tackle gaps concerning the MRCO's vision or strategy
- considering how to strengthen the board's skills – by training the current board members or bringing in new people with skills (eg financial) that are now required
- organising staff training to fill key skill gaps
- introducing more rigorous procedures (eg for controlling money)
- developing policies (eg on equal opportunities or health and safety)
- investing in ICT (eg better telephones, or better accounting software).

African Children's Club – NE London

The African Children's Club, commonly known as ACC, helps young people, mainly of African descent, develop their confidence and self esteem. CEMVO (the Council of Ethnic Minority Voluntary Organisations) assisted ACC through its capacity-building programme. The improvements were implemented by a capacity-building officer who identified the organisation's needs by using a diagnostic toolkit, which analysed nine key areas of development:

- constitution and legal structure
- governance structure and process
- business and action planning
- management systems
- financial systems
- funding
- communication and marketing
- partnership and networking
- information and communication technology

The toolkit resulted in an action plan, which identified and recommended changes required within the organisation. Over the course of a year, regular meetings were arranged so that strategies, policies, procedures, networking and training could all be developed. The officer also monitored progress by collecting evidence on a regular basis, so that ACC could be accredited as having been efficiently 'capacity built'.

Source: www.emf-cemvo.co.uk

What help is available for capacity building?

A rigorous capacity check may well reveal a number of gaps of various kinds which the MRCO will not be able to fill without outside resources. There are many agencies which offer help with capacity building, and this is a rapidly changing field in which local resources might be available to particular groups (eg special help to develop the capacity of BME organisations).

Appendix 2 gives an extensive list of the most relevant organisations and sources of capacity-building help at the time of writing the guide.

One possibility is that a commissioning body itself gives capacity-building help to MRCOs, on the basis that it wants to develop their role as service providers. Or it could finance MRCOs to receive capacity-building help from other agencies. So far, there are few examples, but this is one.

MRCO capacity building in Haringey

Haringey's commitment to promoting the role of BME groups (including MRCOs) in service provision has involved working with groups to strengthen their capacity. For example, in the case of one MRCO providing commissioned services to a particular migrant community, concern about its operations has led to a long period of engagement with its management committee. Agreement has been reached to move the service and staff out to another provider temporarily, bringing in outside advice to strengthen the MRCO's capacity so that it can run the service again, and to encourage greater service user involvement. The borough has also commissioned a piece of research to help it understand the particular community and how it is affected by political divisions in its country of origin.

Further information: www.haringey.gov.uk/sq/index/community_and_leisure/voluntary_sector.htm

Another unusual but potentially very helpful arrangement is a partnership between a small body and a larger one, eg an MRCO and a housing association working together as Supporting People providers, the one helping to build the capacity of the other (with the association imparting knowledge about SP, while gaining knowledge about culturally sensitive service provision from the MRCO). An example of a larger third sector body helping smaller ones is Olmec.

Olmec's Solid Foundations and Nexus programmes

Olmec is a subsidiary of Presentation Housing Association, set up to develop the capacity of community-based organisations, especially those working in BME communities. Through its Solid Foundations programme, it works with RCOs to secure placements and relevant training for their staff, often with Presentation HA.

It also has a programme called Nexus which arranges 'pro bono' (or free) advice by businesses to local third sector bodies. For example, Devonshires (the solicitors) gave legal advice and training workshops to the Iranian and Kurdish Women's Rights Organisation.

More information: www.olmec-ec.org.uk

Source: hact (2006) *An Opportunity Waiting to Happen: Housing Associations as 'Community Anchors'*.

How do quality assurance systems relate to capacity building?

Quality assurance systems are designed to help organisations perform efficiently by setting and monitoring standards for specific aspects of running an efficient organisation. These 'quality areas' may include governance, management, finance, administration and other aspects of the organisation's capacity. For each aspect, a standard is defined, along with specific criteria that determine whether the organisation is meeting the standard.

Quality assurance is therefore complementary to capacity building in providing a way of demonstrating (eg to a commissioning body) that an MRCO has reached a certain quality standard (or level of capacity).

The systems may be based on self-assessment or on accreditation. There is also a separate category of quality assurance systems that relate to particular services:

Self-assessment based systems

These are used by organisations themselves to assess how well they meet specified standards. Because they depend entirely on the organisation's own commitment and efforts, self-assessment systems, when used consistently throughout an organisation, are powerful tools for encouraging the board, staff and volunteers to assess and promote high standards of operation and service delivery, but have the disadvantage of not providing an independent accreditation.

There are a number of self-assessment systems currently in use by voluntary organisations:

- *PQASSO (Practical Quality Assurance System for Small Organisations)* is the most widely known (http://www.ces-vol.org.uk/). It provides standards in 12 quality areas, accompanied by checklists of criteria for meeting each of three levels of achievement in a specific area. Action plan templates are provided so that organisations can record and plan measures to improve performance.
- *Quality First* (www.bvsc.org/development/quality-first.html) is a simple, free tool that was specifically designed for community organisations with no paid or only part-time staff. Its nine quality areas reflect the nature of community groups and their activities.
- *QASRO (Quality Assurance System for Refugee Organisations)*[81] is designed for (and by) voluntary organisations working with asylum seekers and refugees. It too specifies standards for key aspects of running an organisation. Some of

---

81 Information is available from the Refugee Council (see www.refugeecouncil.org.uk/practice/support/quality.htm).

these, such as diversity and equality, reflect the particular concerns of refugee organisations. Checklists of criteria for each standard are supplemented by examples of specific evidence that can be used to assess achievement. Unique features of QASRO are its guidelines on delivering five key refugee services, and its collection of sample policies and other materials to help organisations set up and improve their operations. QASRO also signposts organisations to a wide range of other resources and information.

Accredited systems

In contrast to self-assessment based systems, accredited systems rely on assessment by an external body that, for a fee, decides whether standards are met. Organisations which successfully complete the assessment process are awarded an accreditation (or 'kitemark'). Well-known accredited systems include Investors in People (www.investorsinpeople.co.uk) and the **matrix** standard (www.matrixstandard.com). While both systems cover all aspects of running an organisation, Investors in People emphasises training and staff development while the **matrix** standard is designed for organisations delivering information, advice and guidance.

Service-based accreditation systems

There are specific systems that apply to particular services or that are administered or required by commissioning bodies. Two that are already familiar to many MRCOs are Quality Mark, a system for advice services administered by the Legal Services Commission, and the kitemark of the OISC (Office of the Immigration Services Commissioner), the body which regulates immigration advice (both are discussed in chapter 14). Other systems are referred to in the appropriate chapters in part two of the guide.

Quality Mark training by MODA

MODA offered a special five-day one-to-one training session to the co-ordinator and management committee members of Anatolia (Turkish-Kurdish) Community Organisation in Hackney. This is a well-established group which provides services relating to immigration, employment, housing, education and general community development to Turkish-speaking communities.

The aim of the training was to develop the organisation's systems and structure as well as the knowledge and skills of its workers, so that the organisation could apply for and obtain the Quality Mark.

Further information: www.moda.org.uk

South London Tamil Welfare Group (SLTWG) and the Quality Mark

'SLTWG applied for the Quality Mark in 2000. Many funders were asking for this as a requirement, and we also wanted to show that we were providing a quality and accredited service. We already had a lot of the requirements in place, like staff supervision and file management, but these were quite varied as they reflected a wide range of projects and the monitoring requirements of different funders. Our main task was bringing everything together and adapting it, and we found the checklist very useful.

'Having the Quality Mark has improved our management structure and made us more systematic, and also helped with fundraising. It has also enhanced our confidence with clients, as we follow very set procedures which have been externally assessed, so we can be sure we are giving a good service. I and the co-ordinator are responsible for implementing and monitoring how the procedures are working, with regular visits from external assessors. We applied for exemption from the OISC at the same time as doing the Quality Mark, and applied for support from external agencies like FIAC and the Refugee Council.

'Achieving the Quality Mark is a lot of work for all staff, but it is very useful. The difficulty is trying to achieve a balance between maintaining the quality of the service and the high level of demand from the community. The only difference clients experience is that they have to wait longer to access our services now, and this has put us in a difficult position. The only way to overcome this is to increase our human resources to deliver services. At the end of the day, the community trusts us whether we are accredited or not as we have been giving advice for 17 years.

'My advice to other organisations considering it would be to go ahead, but be aware of the impact on staff time, and to ensure someone in the organisation is responsible for implementing and continual monitoring. Getting the systems in place is the hardest bit; once everything is up and running there is less pressure. Overall it has been positive – it shows clearly what the organisation does, how we deliver our services and that we are approved and accredited.'

Source: Dr Anthony Kingsley, project manager for SLTWG, quoted in *RCO News*, Issue No 8, March 2003

It is also wise for commissioning bodies to acquaint themselves in some detail with the main quality assurance systems so that they know what they signify when an organisation cites a particular system. It is tempting to rely on accredited systems to provide assurances on quality, but a comprehensive portfolio of evidence compiled by a QASRO user, for example, might indicate an active, well-embedded commitment to quality if a commissioner knows enough about quality systems to ask for it.

Chapter 8

Commissioning Bodies' Role in Promoting MRCOs

What this chapter is about
- how commissioning bodies can become more open to MRCOs
- identifying refugee and migrant-related service needs
- how commissioning processes can be changed
- identifying barriers that deter MRCOs
- how contracts can be structured to enable MRCOs to bid more readily
- running contracts in ways that help MRCO providers.

How can commissioning bodies be more open to service provision by MRCOs?

However much MRCOs prepare themselves to become providers of commissioned services, they will only be successful if commissioning bodies are more aware of the role they could play and are open to the possibility of MRCOs being awarded contracts. This chapter looks at the issue from the perspective of the commissioning body and the commissioning process, and is about how the body itself and the processes it operates can be made more receptive to MRCOs (and, in the process, provide better services to refugees and migrants).

An unthinking response to the question posed in the heading (or the wider one about involvement of the third sector in service provision generally) is to say that the tendering process is open and any organisation can compete to provide services. However, as chapter 4 explained, the government has already recognised that such an approach is wrong: third sector organisations, especially BME organisations, need specific encouragement to play a role in service provision. With the importance now attached to the third sector's role, it is not an issue which government departments, commissioning bodies and local authorities can afford to ignore.

The previous chapter argued that commissioning bodies should help to build the capacity of MRCOs to deliver services. This chapter argues that commissioning bodies can encourage MRCOs in three further ways:

- by ensuring that their service provision and contracts fully embrace the areas of need, the types of service provision and the communities that are of interest or concern to MRCOs
- by adapting their commissioning processes so that they are accessible to smaller third sector organisations like MRCOs
- as far as possible, by structuring and running contracts to give more opportunities to bodies such as MRCOs.

Commissioning bodies which are inexperienced in this area, or feel they lack knowledge of appropriate MRCOs, might want to make contact with or collaborate with other local bodies that are in a similar position, or with bodies that are already known to work with MRCOs and who might be willing to share their experience.

Many of the points in this chapter relate equally to other BME organisations or small service providers, not just MRCOs. They therefore have wider relevance to the government's agenda of promoting the role of the third sector, and particularly of small providers. They are also important in relation to the requirements on commissioning bodies to meet equality and diversity objectives (and comply with legal obligations to promote good race relations) in their service provision.

Are services appropriate for asylum seekers, refugees and new migrants?

MRCOs are well-placed to provide services to marginalised groups such as these – but can only be commissioned to do so if the commissioning body recognises that the needs exist and builds its services accordingly. How can this be done, within the framework of the commissioning process?

Government advice on taking account of social needs

Government guidance says that commissioners should be aware of the government's social priorities – which could include (for example) its refugee integration strategy.[82] They should identify which policies are relevant to the commissioning they are undertaking, and what scope there is to take them into account. As pointed out in chapter 3, commissioning bodies can also explicitly consider social issues in the

---
82 Home Office (2005) *Integration Matters*.

commissioning process providing they do this at the right stage – in setting requirements in the contract specification.

Government advice says:[83]

> 'Consider social issues at the outset. There is most scope available early on in the process, in the business case or when defining needs and specifications, and early action is more likely to be successful.'

While this advice is sound, inevitably many commissioning bodies are already running a cycle of contracts, and in practice identifying and 'feeding in' newly identified needs has to fit in with this cycle and may well need time to take full effect. Also, commissioning bodies cannot simply add social elements into the contract without careful evaluation and justification of any additional costs. Government is currently looking at the barriers to putting 'social clauses' into contracts, so further developments can be expected.[84]

Ways of finding out about social needs

Commissioning bodies which are contracting out client-based services (of the kind that MRCOs might provide) obviously have to make assessments of the needs for those services, and act on feedback from service users, in a continuing cycle of judging the need for and adapting services over time. The specific ways in which the needs of asylum seekers, refugees and migrants might be built into these processes could include:[85]

- *Surveys aimed at finding out the needs of particular groups*, for example, newly established BME groups which might have low awareness of the availability of certain services. Chapter 12 gives the example of Sheffield's strategic review of refugee needs for Supporting People services.
- *Consultation with appropriate bodies* (like MRCOs) that represent those groups. This is perfectly acceptable if done in a way which does not advantage or disadvantage particular suppliers.
- *Using the expertise of MRCOs*, for example, for staff training, to comment on aspects of service specification, including them in advisory panels on services, or funding research by them into service design to meet users' needs.

---

83 Office of Government Commerce (2006) *Social Issues in Purchasing*, p9 (available at www.ogc.gov.uk). The Scottish Government advice on social issues is available on their procurement website (www.scotland.gov.uk/Resource/Doc/116601/0053331.pdf).
84 See Cabinet Office (2006) *Partnership in Public Services: An action plan for third sector involvement*, p23.
85 A useful general discussion of the third sector and the commissioning process is Blackmore, A (2006) *How Voluntary and Community Organisations can help Transform Public Services* (available at www.ncvo-vol.org.uk/). Some of the points here are taken from it.

- *Using surveys by or commissioning them from MRCOs.* This may be a way of finding out about hidden needs. For example, in one London Borough, an RCO conducted a comprehensive survey of its community and was able to present the authority with detailed evidence of housing need. In another, a group working with migrant domestic workers identified their needs – often hidden because they live in their employers' homes in an affluent part of London. An example of a recent survey of this kind is the one by Link Action.

> ### Survey of needs of Somalis in Sheffield
>
> Link Action is a group of Somali volunteers who worked with the Northern Refugee Centre to obtain training sponsored by Active Learning through Active Citizenship (http://togetherwecan.direct.gov.uk/). With the skills they developed they were able to carry out a survey into issues such as the problems faced by young Somali people, and produce a report (available at www.alacsy.org.uk) directed at social services and education authorities.

- *Using more general survey data on refugees and migrant groups.* A major difficulty in identifying needs is the under-representation of refugees and migrants in the census and similar surveys. However, there is a growing body of ad hoc research on their needs, and the extent to which they are marginalised by public services.[86] There is also evidence of specific needs such as those of women[87] or destitute asylum seekers.[88] (Needs surveys are too numerous to mention in detail here).

- *Ensuring compliance with equal opportunities (and particularly race relations) legislation.* Commissioning bodies should ensure that their specifications or user requirements reflect relevant legislation, especially that on race and ethnicity (see chapter 4). Where relevant to the service, contracts might include a requirement that service providers must meet the needs of all BME groups, not just long-established ones, or specify an 'outcome' that the levels to which services are used by particular groups in the community are raised. (Not to take this kind of action is to risk intervention by the Equality and Human Rights Commission.)

---

[86] For example, in relation to health, a study of refugee primary care needs (www.networks.nhs.uk/uploads/06/06/refugees_in_primary_care.doc). For various local and national studies on migrants' needs, see the reviews on the hact website (www.hact.org.uk/downloads.asp?PageId=173).

[87] See for example the Why Women campaign to gain a bigger role for women's third sector bodies (www.whywomen.org.uk).

[88] An example is the report by Refugee Action and Leicester Asylum Seekers and Refugees Voluntary Sector Forum in 2005 (available at http://refugee-action.org/news/destitutionreport.aspx).

- *Carrying out an equality impact assessment*[89] so as to assess the likely impact of the planned commissioning on particular ethnic minorities and other groups, ensuring of course that the research adequately covers the needs both of more recent migrants and of longer-established BME communities.

Through steps like these, commissioning bodies can gain evidence on which to base the requirements in their contract specifications.

Consulting on the range of needs to be met

If a commissioning body carries out research or survey work to determine needs, it is good practice to consult with interested groups and the wider public on the results of such work and the range of needs the body plans to meet, with any expressions of priority between them (see example below).

London Councils consults on community needs

London Councils, which represents and distributes grants on behalf of London boroughs, has consulted on the range of needs that should be met from the grants programme in future. These include:

- advice services (including employment-related advice) to refugees and migrant communities
- programmes to increase refugee involvement in sports and cultural activities
- advice services to improve refugees' access to health services.

The priorities were assessed on the basis of consultation with a wide range of groups, and the results are themselves subject to further consultation as the basis for the 2006/07 funding programme, which is based on the principle of commissioning services rather than awarding grants.

More information: www.londoncouncils.gov.uk/

Setting specifications that reflect the needs of asylum seekers, refugees and migrants

It is impossible to give a comprehensive list of ways in which the needs of asylum seekers, refugees and migrants might be reflected in specifications, because they will differ from service to service. But some examples could be:

---

[89] See the CRE pages on such assessments (http://83.137.212.42/sitearchive/cre/duty/reia/index.html).

- *Extending the list of language requirements* for a service to include languages spoken by new migrant groups as well as long-established community languages, eg requiring that a certain proportion of staff are fluent in speaking and writing Arabic (and able to give advice and deal with documents in that language).

- *Requiring services to be delivered in culturally sensitive ways* – to address the needs of particular sections of the community, including (for example) people who are newly arrived in the UK, or women from particular BME groups where there is evidence of lower usage of certain services (see box).

- *Specifying locations for services* that will make them more accessible to particular communities (eg advice services), but without introducing unfair requirements (eg that the provider is a local organisation).

- *Requiring 'community buy-in' to a service* which helps to strengthen the community's capacity or helps regenerate an area.

- *Requiring staff awareness* of issues such as the sensitivities of dealing with clients whose immigration status is uncertain, or who have just left temporary accommodation for asylum seekers, including a requirement for appropriate training of staff having face-to-face contact with clients.

- *Identifying particular needs* likely to be more evident in the refugee community, such as mental health problems associated with trauma, the needs of torture victims, etc that might not be met by conventional services.

- *Defining 'hard-to-reach' groups* (including refugees and migrants) and asking for evidence of how the service provider will provide services to them.

- *Asking for evidence of user involvement* – how the service provider will secure it and respond to user views.

Building in an outcome to gain more female service users

Research, monitoring or community feedback might show to the commissioning body that a particular service was under-used by ethnic minority women in an area, and as a result it might include an outcome in its specification that service usage by those groups be increased by a certain percentage. It would then be up to providers to show how they might achieve this requirement, eg by separate facilities for women, by having women staff from the same ethnic background, by working with appropriate women's groups in the areas, etc. BME community organisations such as MRCOs might have particular local knowledge and skills to enable them to meet the requirement.

An example of the kind of study, in consultation with MRCOs, that might be used to inform the specification of services (in this case, mental health) is *Unheard Voices: Listening to refugees and asylum seekers in the planning and delivery of mental health service provision in London*.[90]

How can the commissioning process be made more accessible to MRCOs?

Government advice[91] urges commissioning bodies to plan the commissioning process carefully and 'ensure it is accessible to a suitable variety of suppliers', including the third sector and BME enterprises. This should be based on 'early dialogue' with suppliers, including social enterprises and the third sector.

Government argues that doing so is likely to increase competition and therefore improve value for money, and potentially provide more innovative and responsive services, eg for 'hard-to-reach' groups and deprived communities. The aim should therefore be to ensure that third sector bodies and BME enterprises can compete on a 'level playing field' with other suppliers.

Ways in which this might be done include:

- *early, informal consultations* with providers, potential providers and sector representatives to better understand the market and the role they play in it
- *reviewing the information on contracts* to make sure it is accessible to small providers – for example, some commissioning bodies have developed plain English guides to the commissioning process which they put on their websites
- *awareness raising* with third sector and BME bodies so that they know about developments in commissioned public services, changes in contracting requirements, tendering timetables, requirements they would have to meet as providers, etc
- *advertising* contracts in local media or through appropriate networks to which such groups would have access (as well as trade media, or adverts to meet EU competition requirements)
- *having a named contact* within the commissioning body, responsible for liaison with third sector and BME providers
- *hosting events for current and potential service providers* to encourage interaction between smaller and bigger providers (that might lead to collaboration, such as through subcontracts)

---

90   Palmer, D and Ward, K (2006) (available at www.irr.org.uk/pdf/Unheard_Voices.pdf).
91   OGC (2006) *Social Issues in Purchasing*, p9.

- *developing the capacity of MRCOs* through grants or other means (see chapter 7)
- *market testing* in ways which include the third sector and BME sectors (but do not exclude other sectors)
- *informing* MRCOs of bodies which may be able to help them, such as those mentioned in appendix 2
- *training* appropriate groups to increase their skills and competitiveness in completing tender documentation
- *accrediting* suppliers (or creating 'approved lists') and providing guidance on how to get accredited and the standards required (see below)
- *getting feedback* from potential providers who do not actually bid, to find out about any obstacles they met
- *giving feedback* to failed bidders, to help them in the future.

Some commissioning bodies may have an accreditation scheme for providers, or an approved list of tenderers, and only organisations that qualify for inclusion are able to submit tenders. In some cases, there may be provision for an 'interim' status for new providers enabling them to gain a provisional contract which is confirmed when their accreditation is achieved. Also, there may be 'passporting' arrangements, whereby a provider accredited by a second body (or a national scheme like PQASSO – see chapter 7) is judged to meet all or some of the criteria applied by the first body.

Accreditation Scheme – Sheffield's Supporting People programme

The scheme (which is based on CLG national requirements for SP) has five criteria relating to:
- financial viability
- administrative procedures
- employment policies
- management procedures
- track record.

Most of these are self-assessed through a questionnaire (which is then validated for accuracy). There is provision for new providers without a track record to demonstrate in other ways that they are in a position to provide a good service. Providers which are already accredited by other bodies can be passported through some of the requirements.

More information: www.sheffield.gov.uk/safe--sound/supporting-people/information-for-providers

What barriers might exist which discourage MRCOs?

Barriers to greater participation by MRCOs are generally of two kinds:

- those on the commissioning body side, which can potentially be changed as part of the commissioning process (considered here)
- those on the MRCO side – lack of resources, knowledge or skills on the part of the MRCOs – which the commissioning body can help to remedy through capacity building (see chapter 7).

Commissioning bodies should check that their practices do not discriminate against particular groups of providers or potential providers – in particular, BME providers such as MRCOs, or client groups such as migrants or refugees. This could be done as part of an equality impact assessment – see above.

It is important to ensure that commissioning does not inadvertently exclude MRCOs by imposing requirements that are not strictly relevant and which may create obstacles to their participation. Commissioners should be aware of inappropriate attitudes towards these client groups, or inappropriate assumptions, eg that MRCOs might be transitory and therefore not secure long-term providers.

To satisfy their own equal opportunities policies, they may want to collect information on the characteristics of those winning contracts, so that they have a better profile of their providers and know their backgrounds. This could include finding out whether any of them are ethnic minority businesses (while making clear that this will not affect contract decisions).[92]

If an assessment shows that small BME providers (for example) are under-represented, then finding ways of providing more opportunities for them could increase the value for money obtained from the commissioning process. Commissioning bodies also need to ask themselves whether they are prejudiced against providers such as MRCOs – even long-established ones might be thought to have no 'track record' or to be less reliable than larger providers, without any evidence that this is the case. At the same time, one supplier (or type of supplier) must not be favoured over another, at any stage of the process, even if they are from an under-represented group.

Some of the barriers which might be identified are these:

- *Requiring too much detail.* In setting requirements, commissioning bodies should bear in mind that organisations such as MRCOs often do not have the

---

[92] A way of doing this is suggested in the CRE procurement guide, p69.

capacity to provide lots of detailed information where it is disproportionate or irrelevant to delivery of the contract. Requirements should be considered carefully so as not to disadvantage bodies like MRCOs. For example, it is good practice to ask only for two years of accounts,[93] and not to expect small charities (with turnover under £100,000) to comply with other than simple accounting arrangements.

- *Having only large contracts or being biased towards known providers*. Large contracts help get economies of scale, but may reduce the supplier base by driving out small suppliers who could add value in other ways. A similar danger is that the commissioning body is (probably unconsciously) oriented towards established providers, rather than encouraging newer (probably smaller) ones.

- *Setting geographical boundaries which affect some potential providers more than others*. MRCOs often operate across local authority boundaries (eg in London, across several boroughs). It may be difficult for them to supply specialist services to one authority alone, and joint commissioning may therefore be appropriate for some services:

    'Evidence shows that commissioning specialist services at the local level can sometimes limit the ability of specialist third sector providers (along with specialist providers from other parts of the independent sector) to bid for contracts.'[94]

- *Treating large contractors in the same way as small ones*. It may be appropriate to differentiate between larger and smaller contracts (the ones MRCOs are more likely to bid for), and adopt more limited requirements for the latter.

- *Setting onerous experience requirements*. Such experience requirements could not be met by recently established MRCOs, and should only be included if really justifiable.

- *Setting short contract periods*. Commissioning bodies may feel under pressure to re-tender frequently in order to keep costs down – but if this puts off bodies like MRCOs it may be counter-productive. Government policy is now that 'funding of at least three years becomes the norm rather than the exception'.[95]

- *Having inappropriate divisions of risk*. Risk should be carried by the body best able to deal with it – placing excessive risk on small providers may deter them from bidding.

---

93 OGC (2004) p22.
94 Cabinet Office (2006), p21.
95 Cabinet Office (2006), p28.

- *Making specifications too prescriptive of delivery methods*. As mentioned above, outcome-based specifications may encourage MRCOs to develop new solutions.
- *Setting over-tight timetables*. Voluntary bodies may need time to complete complex tender documents that larger providers are equipped to deal with quickly.
- *Adopting complex legal requirements*. They should be proportionate to the significance of the contract and kept as simple as possible.
- *Not allowing for full cost recovery*. Commissioners may be unfamiliar with full cost recovery (see chapter 9) or assume that third sector bodies can use charitable funding to meet overhead costs.
- *Using payment methods that deter small providers*. There is now considerable guidance on payment arrangements which encourage third sector suppliers – such as accounting for their full costs, and making advance payments to bodies with little capital – with which commissioning bodies should be familiar.[96]
- *Cutting budgets in ways which particularly affect smaller providers*. Despite government advice to the contrary, many Supporting People providers have had to accept budgets which fail to take account of inflation, which small providers find more difficult to cope with than large providers.
- *Not setting requirements about user feedback or involvement*. This can disadvantage potential providers such as MRCOs, one of whose advantages should be their 'closeness' to users.

There is nothing to prevent commissioning bodies consulting third sector groups, including MRCOs, on the needs identified, the services planned, and the commissioning process for delivering them, prior to the tendering process. This will enable feedback to be provided and any barriers to be identified before the formal process begins, as well as being helpful in raising the awareness of potential providers. Such consultation is increasingly a policy commitment.[97]

An example of a commissioner identifying the potential for small community-based providers (including MRCOs) to meet needs that could not so readily be met by larger providers is the LB of Haringey. The example shows how they built the necessary support and capacity building into the contract arrangements.

---

96   See OGC (2004) p25 and the advice at www.government-accounting.gov.uk
97   See for example DH (2006) *No Excuses: Embrace partnership now* (available at www.dh.gov.uk).

Haringey's support for small BME-led service providers

Haringey's Supporting People team identified support needs among minority groups that they felt could best be met by community-based providers, who they would need to support if they were to deliver their contracts. The SP team therefore entered a Service Level Agreement with the council's Corporate Voluntary Sector Team (CVST). CVST provide developmental support and manage and monitor SP contracts with 12 small providers, including several MRCOs, on behalf of the SP Team.

The CVST's activities include:
- guidance for organisations to complete and submit SP documentation
- identifying funding opportunities for groups and assistance with funding bids
- promoting training opportunities and encouraging best practice
- identifying weaknesses within service provision and ensure long-term sustainability of the organisation
- monitoring on a risk-assessment basis (red, amber and green)
- responding to and actioning day-to-day enquiries from organisations
- making and monitoring SP contract payments to organisations
- reconciling budgets; assessing audited accounts and annual reports
- maintenance of financial, administrative and monitoring systems.

Where appropriate, SP monitoring requirements have been amalgamated with internal monitoring systems to reduce the burden on those providers.

The providers are contracted to support 302 people but the estimated number of people actually being supported is 719. In funding terms, £900,000 is invested in these services – 3.2 per cent of the entire SP programme.

Further information: www.haringey.gov.uk/sq/index/community_and_leisure/voluntary_sector.htm

A note of caution is required, too: one RCO interviewed for this guide pointed to the danger of groups 'promising the earth' to commissioning bodies, because they are so keen to win contracts. Obviously, making unrealistic promises is in the interests of neither side in the commissioning process.

Can contracts be structured so as to give more opportunities to MRCOs?

In commissioning a large programme such as Supporting People, there are various ways in which contracts can be structured so as to provide opportunities to MRCOs.

One way is to identify specific types of service or service outcomes applying to a proportion of the services being contracted, or applying to parts of the area being covered. This might provide opportunities to bodies with particular skills (eg delivering culturally sensitive services to particular client groups).

Another way is by packaging contracts in different sizes, so that small providers are given opportunities alongside larger ones. This must be done carefully so as not to violate EU competition rules (which prohibit packaging simply as a means of getting contracts below the sizes at which the rules apply). It must also satisfy the overall value-for-money test. This might be achieved if a large provider is meeting overall needs, whereas a small provider such as an MRCO is providing for the needs of a niche market (an additional level of service required by a particular client group).

Subcontracting

Subcontracting is a key way in which MRCOs might be able to gain entry to providing commissioned services, but without the full risk of running a contract directly. Although the EU competition rules do not allow commissioning bodies to *require* that a contractor uses a particular subcontractor, it is often possible to work with providers to encourage subcontracting.[98] This is now recognised in the government's action plan:[99]

'In many public service areas, contracts are increasingly being awarded through a prime contractor model, whereby a lead organisation offers sub-contracts to other, typically smaller, organisations. In the right circumstances, this can allow these smaller and often specialist suppliers to access markets from which they would otherwise be excluded.'

Ways of promoting subcontracting include:

- Potential providers being told in advance that the commissioning body welcomes the participation of small providers such as MRCOs.
- They could be asked to show in what ways they will achieve value for money, for example by making use of small providers like MRCOs.
- The specification could include making services accessible to people with particular language or other needs.
- Where relevant to the contract, they could be asked to show their proposals for engaging with community organisations such as MRCOs.
- Successful tenderers could be asked to consider subcontracting to bodies such as MRCOs after they have been awarded the contract.

---
98 See OGC (2006) *Social Issues in Purchasing*, p24, OGC (2004) p21.
99 Cabinet Office (2006), p19.

Subcontracting also carries risks. As one MRCO interviewed for the guide said, 'what they want is to pass on all the headaches of the contract to us'. There is therefore an issue about commissioners finding ways to ensure that subcontractors are treated fairly. JCP and DWP have recently undertaken a major tendering exercise involving subcontracting, for delivery of New Deal services, the results of which are being monitored. The Office of the Third Sector is also committed to finding ways of improving the arrangements for subcontracting.[100] This is therefore an area in which changes can be expected soon.

Consortia

Another possibility is that MRCOs might form consortia to bid for contracts. These are attractive to small bodies which otherwise could not compete for contracts. They also help to increase collaboration and reduce competition between bodies like MRCOs. Again, the commissioning body could make it clear that it is open to such bids, or even help the process by linking smaller third sector bodies with larger ones. If successful, consortia may be particularly well-placed to collect data on needs and to influence future service provision for their client groups. More information on consortia and how MRCOs might form them is given in the next chapter.

Running contracts in ways that help MRCO providers

Finally, it is not enough for the commissioning body to have awarded contracts to MRCOs – they now need to consider how they (like any other provider) can be helped to provide a consistent and sustained service that meets the user requirements.

Factors to be considered include:
- Avoiding onerous reporting requirements that place too big a burden on small providers – focus on assessing outcomes.
- Being proactive in working with providers to acknowledge and solve problems (see Haringey example on page 96).
- Avoiding asking for performance information in forms that are different from other commissioning bodies.
- Keeping contract changes to a minimum and giving as much notice of them as possible.
- Being aware of the potential vulnerability of small providers to reductions in services that affect their income.
- Being open to innovation on the part of providers, particularly if new or changing needs are identified.
- Building in user monitoring and feedback.

---

100 Cabinet Office (2006), p21.

A particular priority for small MRCOs which are starting out as service providers is likely to be the payment arrangements and their cashflow. The guide *Think Smart!* contains advice on making advance payments, having frequent payment 'milestones' and ensuring that payments are prompt; it also refers to the appropriate accounting rules.[101]

Checklist on commissioning bodies' role

- ✓ have you considered if a contract can include social needs?
- ✓ how will you identify them?
- ✓ do user requirements reflect the needs of asylum seekers, refugees and migrants?
- ✓ have you made contact with MRCOs and have you consulted them?
- ✓ does your commissioning process encourage small providers such as MRCOs? – what more could you do?
- ✓ are you familiar with, and have you followed, government guidance on encouraging the third sector and, in particular, BME service providers?
- ✓ are any requirements that you impose proportional to the size of the provider?
- ✓ have you checked to see if the procurement process has any other barriers that might be removed or made less onerous? – and have you taken action accordingly?
- ✓ have you structured contracts so that they work for small organisations, for example by encouraging subcontracting?
- ✓ do you give helpful feedback to unsuccessful bidders?
- ✓ will you run the contract in such a way that an MRCO which is a service provider can deliver an effective and sustainable service?

---

101 OGC (2004), p25 (and www.government-accounting.gov.uk).

Chapter 9

Getting Started – What MRCOs can do to become Service Providers

What this chapter is about
- getting started and ways of entering the market
- overview of the commissioning process
- before making a bid
- making a bid
- delivering the contract

The potential commissioning 'market' is huge – central government alone spends over £13bn per year. Chapter 5 gives an idea of the range of such commissioned services, and fuller details are in part two of the guide.[102]

This chapter is for MRCOs who have carried out the kind of self-appraisal described in chapter 6, and have decided to follow the 'commissioning' route in some form. The chapter aims to help them decide how to 'get started' and how to engage with commissioning. MRCOs which have decided to look at providing services in a particular area (eg health) should then read the appropriate chapter in the next part of the guide.

Being aware of the market

A first step for any MRCO is to become aware of developments, as the market is constantly changing. For example (as mentioned in chapter 8), London Councils has decided to move towards commissioning instead of grant funding for the third sector in London, and such opportunities will be more common as local authorities pursue the government's 'modernisation' agenda (see chapter 4). Many government

---

102 See also the wider opportunities outlined in the government's action plan – Cabinet Office (2006), chapter 3.

departments have strategies for commissioning and for third sector involvement, referred to throughout this guide, and these have and will have constant effects on each service area.

If interested in a particular market, MRCOs should keep themselves aware of how it is changing – make early contact with the commissioning body, ensure they are consulted on service developments or assessments of new needs, and check websites or use personal contacts to keep track of the commissioning process.

MRCOs are likely to operate in smaller, niche markets, compared with the big providers, delivering services relevant to the client groups and communities they represent. This means that MRCOs can themselves shape the market – they can identify new service needs, or show that there are 'hard-to-reach' client groups that miss out on current services. Influencing the types of services purchased by commissioning bodies was dealt with in chapter 8.

What is the MRCO's market position?

Before considering making a bid for a contract, an MRCO needs to step back and fully consider its 'market position', and what it needs to do to be ready to enter a market. Here is a possible checklist.

Checklist for before entering a market

- ✓ what are the organisation's strengths and main 'selling points' in the particular service area?
- ✓ what is its reputation?
- ✓ does the relevant commissioning body know it exists?
- ✓ who are the competitors likely to be?
- ✓ who are the key decision-makers in the commissioning body and what are they looking for?
- ✓ what are the recent developments in the service concerned that ought to inform the bid?
- ✓ should the bid be for the whole market or part of it?
- ✓ would it be better to be a subcontractor?
- ✓ what resources are needed to allow a proper bid to be made?
- ✓ how can quality be guaranteed and service delivery monitored?

Ways of entering the market

Entering the market can be done in various ways, and it is impossible to anticipate all the possible routes that an MRCO might take. Most of this chapter is about directly bidding for contracts, but in chapter 8 the guide considered other ways in which commissioners could encourage small organisations like MRCOs in becoming service providers, such as entering or forming a consortium, or becoming a subcontractor to another provider.

In fact, in preparing the guide we have found examples of four different ways in which MRCOs have moved beyond providing services which are just based on grant income. These can be thought of as 'stepping-stones' towards commissioning:

A 'shop' service

A common example is of MRCOs recognising interpretation or translation needs, and offering a service to a local authority, to housing associations or to other potential users such as local solicitors. This may itself lead to a formal contract on a more permanent basis, but may start on the basis of payments per client or per hour of work. The North of England Refugee Service (NERS) interpretation and translation service operates on this basis.

Such local needs may lead to 'one-off' contract opportunities that are not part of the national programmes on which this guide focuses. This happened in relation to translation needs among housing providers in East London (see box), where as a result a social enterprise (a co-op) was created.

> ### Interpreter/translation service based on local language skills[103]
>
> In partnership with five other associations, Newlon HA helped establish the ARTICLE service to provide quality interpreter and translation services. They assessed their needs and their existing costs, and decided that it would be cost effective to set up a dedicated service based on the skills of their tenants. This required potential interpreters to complete a training course. ARTICLE is now a co-op, with a part-time co-ordinator, offering services to the housing sector throughout this part of London, outside normal hours if required.
>
> The ARTICLE service has won awards, including a National Housing Award in 2004, and Newlon have published a guide to help other organisations set up similar services.
>
> More details: info@articletranslation.co.uk or regeneration@newlon.org.uk

---

103 Quoted from Perry (2005), p65.

A one-off contract

A contractual arrangement which is not the result of a bidding process (sometimes therefore called a 'service level agreement') might be entered into by a larger organisation which recognises that an MRCO can provide particular services to its customers (eg advice services in a minority language) which it cannot easily provide itself.

A subcontract

This is an agreement between a main contractor and a second organisation, for the execution of part of the contract by the second organisation (the 'subcontractor'). It might apply for example when the main contractor is able to fill legal and financial conditions that the subcontractor cannot, or where the subcontractor has better skills or knowledge in relation to part of the contract (eg language skills). Ways in which commissioning bodies can encourage subcontracting were given in the last chapter. Here are some examples of MRCO subcontracting:

- Manchester Refugee Support Network (details on page 120).
- Wolverhampton's Refugee & Migrant Centre is subcontracted or has SLAs under the Voluntary Assisted Return and Reintegration Programme (VARRP), which is funded by the Home Office and the European Refugee Fund.
- NERS (see above) are subcontracted to provide support under the International Organisation for Migration's Assisted Voluntary Return of Irregular Migrants (AVRIM) programme which assists non-EU citizens, in the UK illegally, who would like help in returning to their country of origin.

A consortium

In the context of commissioning, a consortium is a group of organisations (eg MRCOs) which come together in a formal agreement to bid for and run a contract, typically one which they would find it difficult to compete for on their own. The stages in establishing a consortium might be:

- MRCOs identify potential partners with experience of/interest in the relevant service area (possibly with similar experience as each other but with different ethnic minority/faith/language groups).
- They look for a 'second-tier' or support agency that can help them establish the consortium and prepare to enter the commissioning process (alternatively, a support agency might proactively search for interested MRCOs).
- The group and the support agency consider whether they are strong enough to bid as they are or whether they need to bring other bodies into the consortium.

- The consortium (aided by the support agency) develops a common service model (based on their pooled experience) and a delivery plan.
- They assess their capacity (and where necessary, reinforce it) in terms of the knowledge and skills needed to bid for and to deliver the contract, and their ability to provide ongoing support to the consortium members as the contract rolls out.

An example of a consortium which includes MRCOs is given below.

VC Train in Yorkshire

VC Train is a member organisation for third sector learning providers in Yorkshire and Humberside, including several BME groups and MRCOs (eg El-Nisah, Yemeni Economic & Training Centre and Lifeline Solutions). It provides a structure in which they bid for commissioned services through bodies like the LSC. It is not a consortium in the sense that it bids for contracts itself, but it provides a support framework for small organisations that strengthens their capacity to be commissioned service providers.

More information: www.vctrain.org

Entering the market – a warning

One of the organisations interviewed for this study had an interesting 'story' of how it became a service provider, but it subsequently failed in a major contract. It provides some cautionary lessons for MRCOs entering the market and for commissioners seeking to enter contracts with them.

How one MRCO developed and then failed as a service provider

Some might question whether this organisation was an MRCO at all since it did not appear to develop out of either an informal or formal community membership structure, but was always driven more by developing income-generating services. It could perhaps have more accurately been described as a social enterprise as it was a not-for-profit organisation established by professional activists from one local community, in 2000. It has had various contracts for accommodating asylum seekers.

→

Its initial 'success' could be attributed in part to having strong leaders with personal skills and the confidence to engage with outside organisations. Also the group did not have the governance arrangements which would be expected of registered charities, etc and that apply to many other community-led organisations. They were willing and able to act in a responsive and flexible way – for example, in remote management of properties being used for emergency accommodation – but may not have considered the impact on standards and customer care.

Their first experience was as a subcontractor to a larger organisation, which championed them and helped their credibility with other organisations. Although they valued the experience of having been a subcontractor, they were also aware of the disadvantages, such as the relatively low fees they were paid (although they agreed that the main contractor assumed a lot of the risk).

They then began to take on larger contracts as a sole contractor. However, although experienced, they tried to cut corners. They took risks that they might not have done had they been more closely related to the community base they came from originally, and had their governance structures been stronger. After complaints and a subsequent police investigation, they eventually lost one of their main contracts.

The example provides a warning to MRCOs to ensure that they have strong governance arrangements, and to commissioners not to take for granted the 'community' basis of an MRCO but to check its background in more detail.

An overview of commissioning – typical steps

No one commissioning process is the same as another, but it is possible to give an idea of the stages that it normally follows. These are the typical steps in a commissioning process. They should be read together with the guidance in chapter 3 and the specifics on particular services in part two of the guide.

The rest of this chapter looks at these steps and the action that an MRCO, which wants to be a service provider, will need to take. See the table on the next page.

More detail on commissioning and how to bid is available on the website aimed at small and medium enterprises (www.supply2.gov.uk/) which has various step-by-step guides to the processes. Other detailed sources of guidance on commissioning are given in appendix 1.

Commissioning – steps in the process	
Action by commissioning body	Opportunity for MRCO who wants to bid
Need is identified – through a survey by the commissioning body, change in government policy, or the case being made by an outside body	Can themselves make the case for a new service – or a service to a 'hard-to-reach' group that has previously missed out
Decision to commission the service – a specification is developed	Must be aware of timetable so as to be ready to bid
Market is tested, or possible providers sought	Must have made clear to commissioning body that willing and able to bid
An approved list or system of accrediting providers may be established	Find out what the criteria are and how to meet them; check if there is any 'interim' status available (short of full accreditation) for new providers
Commissioning body sets award criteria – the balance between price and quality	Cannot have access to detail but should find out as much as possible about the way the award will be decided
Contract conditions set	Must be aware of these and take them into account
Contractor appointed	If not a winning contractor, is there scope for a subcontract? Ask for debriefing as to why the contract was placed elsewhere
Contract management begins	Establish a close relationship with the client-monitoring officer and clarify any doubts about the expectations to be met
Payments made to contractor	Be aware of provisions that the commissioning body should be making for payments to a third sector provider (see page 95)
Delivery, quality and any expected service improvements are monitored	Make sure systems are in place to provide information on performance and allow problems to be spotted quickly
Review and re-tender of service when contract ends	Be in a position to use the strength of your experience to win further contracts

Before making a bid

In many cases organisations have to prepare a range of documentation at 'pre-tender' stage. These may typically include:

- *Audited accounts* – which may have to go back three years (although government advice – see page 94 – urges commissioning bodies to be flexible about this).
- *Proof of legal status* – for example, company or charity status. (Groups whose status is unclear, or in transition, are likely to need to clarify it at this point. Groups may need to show that running a contract is compatible with their status – for example, with their charitable objectives.)
- *Public liability insurance.*[104]
- *Performance bonds*[105] – again, an obstacle to third sector providers which commissioning bodies may not need to impose.
- *Details of directors and board members* – to show that the MRCO has the appropriate skills/experience and, where relevant, professional qualifications.
- *Details of methods for measuring and maintaining the quality of customer service.*
- *Equal opportunities records and details of compliance with the Race Relations Act and equalities legislation generally.*
- *Accident book records.*
- *References from other similar public bodies* – where appropriate.

When the commissioning body provides details of its requirements, an MRCO which feels disadvantaged by them or unable to comply with all of them might ask for exemptions from some of the requirements. But this must be done at an early stage, not close to the submission deadline, and will not necessarily secure any change.

Making a bid

When bidding begins, it is important to take full advantage of the time available. Find out the timetable, the form in which the tender is required, and whether any interviews are likely to be held.

---

[104] Insurance covering liability for negligent acts resulting in injury, or death of others, and/or property damage.
[105] A form of guarantee, given by someone entering a contract, that in the event of the terms of the contract not being fulfilled, the client will be able to claim compensation from a third party (eg an insurance company).

Making the business case

As pointed out in chapter 3, the object of making a bid is not to submit the lowest price but to demonstrate good value for money compared with other bids. A good all-round bid will show how it addresses the government's efficiency agenda, how quality will be assured in delivering the contract, what additional value the MRCO will add, and why it should be preferred over other bids – as well as setting a good price. These are factors to consider:

- *Show why awarding the contract to an MRCO helps the commissioning body meet government policy* – for example in using the third sector and a BME organisation, or in delivering the government policy such as its refugee integration strategy. Review and use the different arguments in chapter 4 to help make the case.
- *Be confident of the organisation's capabilities and of its closeness to customers*. Show that the extra risk of commissioning from an untried MRCO is balanced by the 'added value' it will give compared with a conventional service provider. Put on record what the organisation has achieved so far.
- *Assess the risks and show an understanding of how they are apportioned* – between the service provider and the commissioning body. Show how possible problems (eg demand being much lower than expected) will be dealt with.

Getting the price right

The price to be offered is of course the most critical element of the bid. Some of the factors to be taken into account are these:

- *Base the bid on 'full cost recovery'* – part of the Compact between government and the third sector is acceptance of this principle (see box).
- *Allocate costs carefully* – doing so according to established principles will strengthen the bid (see box).
- *Find out about the payment regime* which the commissioning body uses – and whether it follows government guidance on payments in advance to third sector providers.[106]
- *Ensure that all operational costs associated with the service to be provided are taken into account* – including extra costs associated with uncertainty at the start of the contract about guaranteeing the level of service (which might mean providing extra staff time initially), and the costs of 'troubleshooting' as the contract proceeds.
- *Make sure all the commitments made in the bid are costed* – so that they can be met in practice.

---

106 See the guidance *A Summary Guide: Improving Financial Relationships with the Third Sector – Guidance to Funders and Purchasers* (available at www.hm-treasury.gov.uk/media/5/3/guidncefundersummary190506.pdf).

- *Apportion overhead costs properly* – so that the overall costs of a building, management time, etc are reflected in the price that is bid.
- *Obtain advice on complex issues such as VAT* – to ensure that these are properly dealt with and are not an unexpected commitment.

Full cost recovery

Full cost recovery means recovering or funding the full costs of a project or service. In addition to the costs directly associated with the project, such as staff and equipment, projects will also draw on the rest of the organisation. For example, adequate finance, human resources, management, and IT systems, are also integral components of any project or service.

The full cost of any project therefore includes an element of each type of overhead cost, which should be allocated on a comprehensive, robust, and defensible basis.

More advice: NCVO provides detailed guidance on assessing costs at www.ncvo-vol.org.uk/sfp/strategicplanning/ and London Voluntary Service Council at www.lvsc.org.uk/Templates/information.asp?NodeID=95560&i1PNID=90016&i2PNID=90158

Source: www.fullcostrecovery.org.uk

Equal opportunities and community cohesion issues

An MRCO will expect its bid to be considered fairly, in part because the commissioning body is likely to have an equality policy reflecting its legal duties under race relations legislation. At the same time, the MRCO must also be able to show that it, too, is aware of and follows good equal opportunities practices in employment and service delivery, especially if more onerous conditions apply to being a commissioned service provider.[107]

For example, the MRCO may be able to present a convincing case for its ability to deliver services to 'hard-to-reach' communities in a culturally sensitive way. But the commissioning body may well want assurances that it can reach 'minorities within minorities', such as women as well as men, and also disabled people. The MRCO might make reference to the measures it will take (eg its recruitment of women advisers) to enhance its service delivery to all members of the community.

---

[107] The CRE provided guidance to voluntary bodies on meeting the requirements of race relations legislation, but MRCOs also need to take account of other equalities legislation. The CRE was replaced by the new Equality and Human Rights Commission (www.equalityhumanrights.com) from October 2007, and the EHRC will issue wider advice, especially as race relations law is incorporated into general legislation on equality.

As noted in chapter 2 (see page 28), there may also be concerns about using MRCOs as service providers which are identified with only one ethnic minority or faith community. MRCOs may want to anticipate this criticism and address community cohesion issues in their bid, or make clear how they relate to wider communities. For example, many MRCOs which started with a narrow community base now offer services more widely and could demonstrate this from their monitoring records. Some MRCOs have changed their names to reflect this and positively aim their services at refugees, migrants or BME communities generally.

Other considerations

In making the bid there may be a need for legal advice or advice on personnel issues, as the contract will be legally binding and staff conditions of service may be affected by it.

The commissioning body may expect a 'method statement' to be submitted as part of the bid – setting out in detail how the service will be provided. In preparing this, the MRCO obviously has to balance a number of considerations – meeting the user requirements, providing a good service to the right customers, and staying within the costs reflected in the price it is submitting for the contract.

Checklist at bidding stage

- ✓ Be customer-focused – sell the commissioning body what it really wants.
- ✓ Explain the purpose of an MRCO and what 'added value' it brings.
- ✓ Check early on if small or first-time organisations are exempt from any of the pre-tender requirements.
- ✓ Ask for information on the split between price and quality that will be used in judging bids – do as much background research as possible.
- ✓ Do some research into bids made for similar services, perhaps in other areas, to compare prices and quality.
- ✓ Ensure that the bid has enough, clear information on the methods that will be used in delivering the contract and meeting user requirements.
- ✓ Make sure the real costs to the MRCO of delivering the service are known.
- ✓ Check whether a performance bond is required and if any alternative is acceptable.
- ✓ Make the case for how the MRCO can help the commissioning body meet its wider social, economic or environmental objectives.
- ✓ Explore the scope for collaboration with other organisations to make a more realistic bid.
- ✓ Ensure any legal advice is obtained before the bid is finalised.

Based on DTI (2003) *Public Procurement: A Toolkit for Social Enterprises* (see www.berr.gov.uk/index.html).

Delivering the contract

An MRCO that successfully wins a contract must then deliver it. Service to the customer is the crucial issue – and one in which MRCOs should already be experienced. Some of the factors to be borne in mind are these:

- *Ensure the approach is right* – if this is a new contract, put extra effort into the early stages to make sure that the service is provided in the right way, and adapted quickly if it is not as good as it should be.
- *Monitor performance* – start keeping records of service delivery straight away. Check what performance indicators and levels are required in the contract and ensure that information is collected in the right way to show if they are being achieved.
- *Have effective complaint mechanisms* – when things go wrong, make sure this is recorded, there is a rapid response, and someone follows up with the customer.
- *Look for ways to improve the service throughout the contract* – it is unlikely that the service will be 100 per cent from the outset, but by looking at any complaints and why they have occurred, customer service can be continually improved.
- *Tackle weaknesses head on* – don't hide problems or be defensive.
- *Keep users on board* – consult them about the service as it develops.
- *Maintain contact with the contract officer* – he or she will be more comfortable with the relationship if they feel well-informed about progress with the contract and any issues arising.
- *Monitor costs and cashflows* – ensure that the payments arrive in the agreed manner.
- *Support key service delivery staff* – troubleshoot problems such as work overload or lack of adequate support for frontline staff. Be aware of who the key staff members are in determining whether the contract is delivered successfully.
- *Be aware of policy changes* – keep abreast of changes that affect the contract or may affect the renewal of the contract.
- *Prepare for the end of a contract* – be prepared to bid again or to seek new work if there is no prospect of contract renewal.

Finally, make sure that people know about the organisation's successes – if customers are satisfied, make sure this is publicised and the MRCO and the commissioning body share the pride of a 'success story'.

PART TWO

CHAPTER 10

ACCOMMODATION AND RELATED SERVICES

> **What this chapter is about**
> - who 'commissions' accommodation services
> - opportunities for bidding for commissioned services
> - potential for MRCOs
> - examples of MRCOs as service providers
> - factors to be kept in mind and likely requirements
> - where to get more information

Who commissions accommodation services?

The main commissioning body for accommodation services that will be familiar to most MRCOs is now the Borders and Immigration Agency (BIA), which commissions asylum seeker accommodation. (This was previously done by NASS, the National Asylum Support Service.) BIA-commissioned accommodation currently houses around 34,000 asylum seekers whose applications are still being processed.

Despite the importance of the main BIA contracts, however, they are not of great significance in the context of commissioning opportunities for MRCOs. For a start, new five-year contracts were agreed in March 2006, and most of these have been with large, mainly private sector suppliers.

Where more opportunities do occur is in the commissioning, by BIA and by local authorities, of more specialist accommodation. There are two main areas.

Section 4 or 'hard case' support is supplied by BIA, who commission accommodation and very basic services from providers; there are currently about 5,400 such cases. Accommodation for unaccompanied asylum-seeking children ('UASC') is supplied and commissioned by local authorities, who may use a variety of means to provide accommodation and support, including foster care.

Other opportunities may exist in contracting to provide housing services to housing associations or local authorities, eg for short-life properties occupied on temporary lets, or for providing advice services. Such contracts tend to be one-off arrangements that are outside the scope of this guide. However, they can provide a 'stepping-stone' towards bidding for commissioned services, by giving the MRCO experience in running a contract and delivering to specified targets. An example is Balik Arts, which has a contract to provide housing-related advice to Turkish tenants in the Stoke Newington area, on behalf of Genesis Community, part of a large housing association (for more on Balik Arts, see page 151).

What opportunities are there for bidding for commissioned services?

Unlike the main BIA accommodation contracts, there are no large-scale negotiations of more specialist contracts. Opportunities are therefore likely to arise from time to time, at local level, in areas where there is demand for this kind of accommodation and either BIA or the local authority is responding to the demand.

Are there specific opportunities for third sector organisations?

Provision of accommodation is a competitive field and both the commissioning bodies and the providers are under pressure to keep costs down. For the main BIA contracts, most providers are now large-scale private firms operating in several regions. Although other types of accommodation contract are smaller, there are similar cost pressures. Nevertheless, MRCOs with previous experience as accommodation providers may find opportunities to gain contracts.

Are there examples of MRCOs providing commissioned accommodation services?

Yes, but so far limited to organisations with a strongly commercial orientation (more in the social enterprise category than traditional MRCOs). These MRCOs have experienced problems, and the experience of one of them is summarised below.

An MRCO's experience with a major accommodation contract

This organisation grew rapidly from having just a handful of properties to managing several hundred. The expertise of the organisation in the housing needs of refugees and their hard work enabled them to secure management agreements with housing associations, and they had agreements to refer clients for rehousing after the end of their support period. Turnover increased rapidly between 2002 and 2006.

They then invested a huge amount of time and resources in bidding for larger accommodation contracts, and were successful in more than one region. Most of the work was done in-house, but they bought in external expertise to help with checking bids and improving presentation. They did not have extensive prior experience in housing management but their big advantages were their detailed knowledge of the neighbourhoods and spending time in talking to local agencies in the areas where they were bidding.

Unfortunately the new scale of operation proved very demanding: there have been (so far unproven) complaints about service quality and a formal investigation into the organisation's actions, although the organisation does still hold the contracts it was awarded.

The lesson is that providing the full range of services associated with large-scale accommodation contracts may be beyond the current capacity of many MRCOs. Given the complexity of such contracts, partnerships with bigger housing agencies might be the way forward. There are successful examples of MRCO partnerships with housing associations in which the MRCO has provided (for example) culturally sensitive support services. None of these have so far followed a 'commissioning' model, however, but tend to be one-off arrangements responding to mutually agreed client needs.

What factors should MRCOs bear in mind and what requirements will they face?

BIA contracts can be large and demanding, and the competition is often with private sector providers who have considerable experience. There is a history of criticisms about providers under BIA (and previously NASS) contracts, reflecting the tight margins that apply and the temptation to sacrifice service quality in order to stay within budget.

Except for BIA contracts, there are not the same standard requirements in this field as apply to some of the other kinds of commissioned service. But MRCOs wishing to be commissioned in this area are likely to need to have a track record in property management, perhaps having been a subcontractor to a larger landlord such as a housing association. They may have to show ability to procure property, through leasing arrangements with private landlords. They will need to be able to demonstrate efficiency and responsiveness in dealing with accommodation needs at short notice and responding to problems such as disrepair. They will have to meet legal requirements, such as those applying to staff in contact with children.

Since the contract may well assume that they carry the risk of properties being empty ('void'), they need to be sufficiently strong financially to carry that risk (or be very good at managing it and keeping associated costs under control).

How can MRCOs find out more?

Again, there is no central source of information or website as there is with other commissioned services. MRCOs are likely to have to depend on local knowledge, perhaps gained from their contacts with the local authority or housing associations (or with BIA) through other housing-related work.

The BIA issues a periodic newsletter, *Asylum News*, which has details of new developments in asylum and refugee policy generally (to subscribe, email: AsylumCommunicationsTeam@homeoffice.gsi.gov.uk).

Hact has published a study of refugee community organisations and the provision of accommodation services, which highlights the difficulties that can be faced.[108]

---

108 Hact (2002) *The Role of RCOs and Refugee Community Housing Associations in Providing Housing for Refugee and Asylum Seekers*.

CHAPTER 11

PROVIDING INTEGRATION AND EMPLOYMENT SERVICES TO REFUGEES

> **What this chapter is about**
> - the Refugee Integration and Employment Service
> - opportunities for bidding for commissioned services
> - opportunities for third sector organisations
> - potential for MRCOs
> - examples of MRCOs as service providers
> - factors to be kept in mind
> - where to get more information

What is the Refugee Integration and Employment Service?

The Refugee Integration and Employment Service is a BIA support programme for newly accepted refugees. Currently it is still at the pilot stage (called 'Sunrise'), but a national service, starting in England in October 2008, is being commissioned as this guide goes to press.[109] There will be equivalent services in Scotland and Wales.

The programme will make available a standard set of services to all new refugees wherever they live in the United Kingdom – enabling them to 'achieve their full potential, contribute to the community and exercise the rights and responsibilities that they share with other residents'.

The Refugee Integration and Employment Service will consist of three distinct but complementary service components:
- an employment advice service
- a mentoring service
- a general advice and support service

The BIA intends to let contracts on a regional basis, for a period of three years.

---
109 www.bia.homeoffice.gov.uk/asylum/outcomes/successfulapplications/integration/sunrise/

Under the pilot scheme, the work has included:
- housing advice
- entry into employment – usually by arranging contact with Jobcentre Plus and other employment advice providers
- advice on benefits – again, usually through Jobcentre Plus
- other financial advice, such as opening bank or post office accounts
- contact with other services, particularly health and education where this has not already been made or where the refugee moves to another locality
- information about English-language tuition and training opportunities where needed
- opportunities for volunteering and for being mentored, if desired
- information on family reunification
- contacts with community, cultural or faith organisations, if sought.

In the first nine months of operation, some 750 refugees and their families took advantage of the Sunrise pilot schemes.

What opportunities are there for bidding for commissioned services?

Sunrise was a grant-awarding programme, but the national scheme is being fully commissioned, through the regional contracts. The Sunrise programme consisted of four pilot projects, in West London/Croydon, Glasgow, Leeds/Sheffield and Manchester. Each started in 2005 and was originally intended to run for two years. Providers were chosen from national adverts: 37 organisations made bids.

The pilots are being run by a combination of local authorities, MRCOs and refugee-related voluntary sector organisations. It can be expected that the national roll-out will provide opportunities for the third sector but will also attract the interest of larger providers.

In awarding full contracts, BIA expects to operate on a 'full cost recovery' basis. In addition, they will expect successful bidders to have a successful track record of providing services to asylum seekers and refugees – a factor which will place the voluntary sector in a strong position to bid. Commissioning of the services will take a regional approach with a remit for lead providers to show how existing front-line organisations will be included in delivery partnerships. These aspects are being made clear at the initial stages of the commissioning process, on which there is information on the Home Office website (see below).

What potential exists for MRCOs?

As can be seen below, MRCOs are already involved as providers in the Sunrise pilots, both as main providers and as subsidiary providers through SLAs. In the Manchester pilot, there is a specific focus on testing the contribution that MRCOs can make to Sunrise, the results of which will influence the national roll-out.

It should be noted, however, that much of the pilot phase depends on the use of volunteers, and MRCOs are likely to be particularly adept at this. It is not yet clear if a national roll-out will be done in the same way, although apparently volunteering is felt to be an appropriate model.

Are there examples of MRCOs providing Sunrise services?

Yes, but limited so far by the pilot nature of the programme.

Manchester Refugee Support Network

Refugee Action (RA) is delivering the Sunrise pilot in Manchester, in partnership with a refugee-led agency, Manchester Refugee Support Network (MRSN). MRSN is an 'enabling organisation' with a community development approach, managed by representatives from refugee communities.

MRSN has in turn established service level agreements (SLAs – effectively written agreements) with three smaller RCOs focused on particular refugee communities. They were recruited through an open bidding process following a briefing session for RCOs, held locally. The three RCOs are the United Somali Bravanese Community, Tameside African Refugee Association (TARA) and the Eritrean Community of Greater Manchester.

Sunrise clients initially meet an RA caseworker and together they complete the client's PIP. RA refers clients to local services for support if needed. If the client needs support to access services, RA refers the client to the MRSN volunteer advocacy service co-ordinator. The co-ordinator then matches the client with a volunteer advocate who is supported by either MRSN or one of the 3 RCOs, depending on the client's needs for language or community support. Volunteer advocates assist with specific actions that the client and caseworker have agreed.

The three local RCOs recruit and support volunteers who continue the work to deliver the personal integration plans, both on an individual basis and through group briefing sessions with refugees who have a common language. Each local RCO is paid a fee (minimum £5,000 per year) to support their office and other core costs, based partly on their caseload. The RCOs received a certain level of support from the MRSN coordinator, for example in QASRO and in managing volunteers.

Contact: www.mrsn.org.uk

How can MRCOs find out more?

MRCOs wishing to be commissioned in this area should keep themselves informed about the progress of the Sunrise pilots and the current national roll-out. Given that the BIA will be looking to learn from the pilots, interested MRCOs can themselves find out about the experience in the pilots, eg through contact with MRCOs in the four areas.

Information on the Refugee Integration and Employment Service is published on the BIA website (www.bia.homeoffice.gov.uk/asylum/outcomes/successful applications/integration/sunrise/). Information on the commissioning process is on the 'Doing Business with us' section of the Home Office website (http://commercial.homeoffice.gov.uk/News/intergration-employment-contract).

CHAPTER 12

HOUSING-RELATED SUPPORT THROUGH SUPPORTING PEOPLE

What this chapter is about
- Supporting People and what it does
- opportunities for bidding for commissioned services
- special provisions for third sector organisations and BME-related services
- potential for MRCOs and examples of MRCOs as service providers
- factors to be kept in mind
- brief summary of requirements
- forthcoming developments
- where to get more information

What does Supporting People do?

The Supporting People (SP) programme provides 'housing-related support' to enable vulnerable people to live independently in the community. SP services include support to find and move into a suitable property; access welfare benefits; manage the responsibilities of the tenancy agreement and be a good neighbour; liaise with other agencies about housing or tenancy issues; develop domestic and life skills, and emotional support to maintain and develop independence.

People who can be supported by the SP programme include homeless people and those at risk of eviction, vulnerable young people, older people with support needs, people with learning or physical disabilities, ex-offenders, women at risk of domestic violence, people with substance misuse problems, those with HIV/AIDs, and people with mental health problems. Refugees can receive an SP service if they are considered vulnerable in the ways described above. Some agencies providing SP services also provide housing. Others offer support only.

Supporting People is relatively new. It was set up by Communities and Local Government (CLG, previously the Office of the Deputy Prime Minister) to bring together a number of different funding streams. When SP began in 2003, the existing services, known as 'legacy services', were automatically given SP funding. Many of these organisations are still providing SP services today.

The annual budget in England is approximately £1.69bn (2007-08 figures). This money is distributed through local authorities. Each authority employs an SP lead officer (and staff team as appropriate) responsible for identifying the services that are needed locally, contracting with provider organisations to deliver these services and ensuring that the contracted services are of good quality. The lead officer is accountable to the commissioning body (CB), made up of senior officers from the council, PCT and probation service. The CB oversees the strategic direction and priorities of the local SP programme. There has to be a five-year strategy identifying priorities and service gaps, including involvement of stakeholders as part of the process.

The Scottish Government is responsible for implementing SP in Scotland, through grants to local authorities. Current spending is around £400m but from 2008-09 it will no longer be a separate budget, but part of overall local government finance. Strategic planning for SP is linked to the local housing strategy and other local plans for community care, health improvement, social inclusion, etc. Services are subject to quality monitoring, through registration by the Scottish Commission for the Regulation of Care and through contract compliance procedures. The Scottish Government's Supporting People web pages contain information, guidance, newsletters and key contacts in the Scottish Government and in local authorities.[110]

In Wales, SP funding is partly allocated to local authorities for distribution, and partly administered directly by the Welsh Assembly Government (WAG). There are plans to devolve it all to local authorities, as in England, but not until at least 2008.[111]

What opportunities are there for bidding for commissioned services?

Where local authorities have funding available, they are commissioning new services. They may do this by approaching an existing provider of SP services, or a specialist agency who they think will be able to start providing SP services, or through an open tender process. The process an authority chooses will depend on that authority's

---

110 See www.scotland.gov.uk/Topics/Housing/Housing/supportpeople/intro (also see the website of the Supporting People Enabling Unit, www.ccpscotland.org/spunit).
111 For information, see the All Wales Supporting People website (http://www.allwalesunit.gov.uk/index.cfm?articleid=887).

standing orders, the value of the contract and the CB's opinion about the merits of different approaches. Some authorities are also putting *existing* services out to tender – this is likely to become increasingly common practice.

Many SP services are currently provided by small organisations. This means that SP teams have to manage a large number of contracts with many different providers. Some authorities wish to reduce the number of contracts they have to manage and will do this by 'aggregating' services and tendering in 'larger chunks' that are beyond the scope of a small organisation. Some may also feel that aggregating services will bring benefits for service users and/or financial savings.

In these authorities, opportunities for small organisations to work independently may reduce. In response, some small organisations are looking at working together in consortia, subcontracting through larger organisations or even merging. But it is always worth bearing in mind that large providers may need smaller ones to help them meet particular needs.

Are there specific opportunities for third sector organisations?

Supporting People is in principle neutral about whether a service is provided by third sector agencies such as local voluntary and community organisations, larger voluntary agencies and housing associations or by private companies.

As SP is a local authority controlled programme, approaches to working and contracting with the third sector will differ. Although government provides guidance to local authorities about the potential role of the third sector and how authorities can work effectively with it, this is not statutory and authorities are not bound by it. Authorities are bound by a local Compact (see chapter 4) if they have signed up to it, as most have. Likewise there are variations in the approach that each authority takes to full cost recovery.

Are there specific opportunities for BME organisations and for MRCOs?

In principle, yes. SP services need to be accessible to all groups. In some cases authorities believe this can best be done by contracting directly with a BME organisation to provide a culturally sensitive service, such as sheltered accommodation for older people from a specific community. Alternatively, when tendering larger contracts, authorities may require applicants to demonstrate how they will work jointly with, or subcontract to, specialist BME services.

A number of MRCOs 'inherited' SP funding when the programme started. Some have done well within the programme. Others, often very small organisations, have struggled to meet the contractual and monitoring requirements of the SP framework. Some local authorities have found ways to protect such services, for example by arranging for them to be 'taken under the wing' of a larger housing association (or even, in one case, taken within the voluntary sector team of a local authority – see page 96). However, some MRCOs have dropped out of the programme or have been decommissioned.

As unmet needs are identified and as demographic patterns change, local authorities will need to ensure that SP services are accessible to new groups. This should create opportunities for relevant MRCOs to take on contracts, either directly if they can demonstrate that they have the necessary capacity, or through a subcontracting arrangement. Sheffield is one of the authorities that has carried out a review of SP services for refugees and other migrants and its commissioning plan[112] sets out the potential roles for MRCOs.

Examples of MRCOs providing SP services

Many of the MRCOs that already provide SP-funded services are legacy services (see above). Examples of MRCOs holding SP contracts directly (with links to background information) include:

- MAAN Somali Mental Health, which provides specialist support services to address mental health issues in the Somali community in Sheffield (see details at http://www.hact.org.uk/downloads.asp?PageId=129)
- Latin American Women's Aid, London, which runs a refuge providing safe housing and support to women at risk of domestic violence (www.islington.gov.uk/directories/page.aspx?dir=council_services&dir_name=LTSP&docid=0901336c8044d2aa&sectionTitle=)
- Vietnamese Mental Health Services, London – see below.

Vietnamese Mental Health Services (VMHS)

VMHS was established in 1989 to address mental health problems among Vietnamese refugees in London. The project started with some grant funding and initial in-kind support from the NHS. Commissioned/contracted work now represents about two-thirds of its revenues.

→

---

[112] www.sheffield.gov.uk/safe--sound/supporting-people/reference-library/strategies--policies/strategic-reviews--commissioning-frameworks

> VMHS provides a range of mental health services for the Vietnamese community in the UK (estimated to be around 30,000, two-thirds living in London) and has a staff of nine.
>
> Since 1993, VMHS has run a six-bedroom hostel providing accommodation and support for homeless, male Vietnamese psychiatric patients. The hostel is owned by Metropolitan HA who also provide housing management. VMHS provide a care and support package funded through SP. The service includes monitoring for early intervention, medication taking, informal counselling/advice, life skills training, etc.
>
> Their SP contract is administered by LB Lambeth, from whom they received support in making their initial bid. VMHS also received a small grant from hact's SP programme to develop policies and procedures on needs and risk assessment, proper support planning, protection from abuse policy, and lone worker policy. Such policies are needed to comply with an SP contract.
>
> Further information: www.vmhs.org.uk/

In addition, various different MRCOs subcontract to provide services to (and receive support from) the London Borough of Haringey Community and Voluntary Sector team (see pages 81 and 96).

What factors should MRCOs bear in mind?

MRCOs wishing to be commissioned and directly hold a contract will need to demonstrate that they can provide a specialist housing-related support service, that this service is needed locally, and that the intended outcomes for the service will help the authority to meet its wider targets and priorities – for example, targets relating to homelessness, community safety, hospital admissions, etc.

Alternatively, MRCOs wishing to provide services but not hold contracts directly will need to join consortia or form alliances with and 'sell' their knowledge and skills to larger providers who can tender to provide services.

What requirements will they face?

Organisations wishing to hold an SP contract need to demonstrate that they are effectively managed and provide quality services that offer value for money. Although individual local authorities can make their own decisions as to how they will test these requirements, in most cases they are based on the national (CLG) SP Accreditation and Quality Assessment Framework models.[113] Providers will also be required to follow the authority's contract monitoring, reporting and management systems.

Subcontracted organisations will have fewer requirements to meet but will still need to demonstrate that they are a well-run organisation and provide a good service. They will also need to have sufficient internal systems to collate data to pass on to the main contractor in order for the latter to fulfil their contractual reporting requirements.

Are changes likely in the near future?

In June 2007, CLG published its new strategy for Supporting People, *Independence and Opportunity*.[114] This includes specific measures to encourage greater third sector participation in SP, including smaller providers. For example:

- a greater focus on service user involvement
- performance monitoring increasingly focused on outcomes (see diagram on page 34)
- emphasis on full cost recovery (see page 109) and on three-year funding arrangements
- investment in the skills of commissioners
- support for capacity building among potential providers
- measures to help small providers, eg encouraging consortia and 'buddying' arrangements (whereby large providers assist smaller ones).

However, the strategy also says that, probably from April 2009, SP funding will no longer be ring-fenced but will be delivered through the wider Local Area Agreement arrangements (see page 39). Given the funding pressures faced by many local authorities, there are concerns about how vulnerable groups with no statutory right to services, and the providers that support them, will fare when the ring fence is lifted.

When SP started, funding was distributed to each local authority according to how much was already being paid to the legacy services, rather than by a detailed analysis of need. CLG may start a process of redistribution (within the parameters of a maximum 10 per cent increase and 5 per cent decrease per year) in an attempt to 'rebalance' provision. This may well lead to cuts in some areas, but also opportunities in others.

---

113 Examples are available on the Supporting People website (www.spkweb.org.uk). See also the Sheffield example on page 92.
114 CLG (2007) *Independence and Opportunity: Our strategy for Supporting People*.

The greatest concern is that current levels of funding for SP (already lower than when the programme started) are due to be reduced still further over the three years from 2008/09. New policy and practice challenges for all SP providers will include how to participate in Local Area Agreements (see above) and the implications of the developing Individual Budgets/Direct Payments agenda.

SP has also been under review in Scotland and a report will be published on the SP section of the Scottish Government website (see above).

How can MRCOs find out more?

The CLG Supporting People website – www.spkweb.org.uk – contains a considerable amount of information (navigation is quite complex – using the 'search' facility is recommended). The strategy document *Independence and Opportunity* can be accessed from here (www.spkweb.org.uk/Subjects/Supporting+People+Strategy+-+CLG/Independence+and+Opportunity+our+Strategy+for+Supporting+People.htm).

There is also *A Guide to Procuring Care and Support Services* (www.spkweb.org.uk/Subjects/Capacity_building/Procurement+guide+templates.htm) which will assist in understanding the procedures which SP teams follow. The Audit Commission has a dedicated website (www.joint-reviews.gov.uk/money/homepage.html) with guidance on getting better value in commissioning SP services.

Hact has a programme for helping small, community-based or specialist housing support providers to thrive within the Supporting People framework through forming partnerships, consortium bids or other forms of collaborative approaches. For details as this develops, see the hact website (www.hact.org.uk/downloads.asp?PageId=175).

Information on the local position can be obtained from local authority Supporting People teams and by looking at their five-year strategies. Some third sector organisations have built relationships with their local SP team and are aware of upcoming issues, plans and priorities. Many SP teams have local 'provider forums' which act as information exchanges and feed into the local strategy.

Chapter 13

Improving Access to Healthcare

> **What this chapter is about**
> - improving access to healthcare – the issues
> - responsibilities within the NHS
> - opportunities for being commissioned
> - practice-based commissioning – what it means
> - the commissioning process
> - potential for MRCOs and examples of MRCOs as service providers
> - brief summary of requirements
> - where to get more information

Why do refugee and migrant communities find it difficult to access healthcare?

Refugees and migrants meet a number of obstacles in accessing good healthcare, including:[115]

- Language and cultural differences.
- Lack of awareness of the way healthcare is delivered in the UK – which is different from home countries.
- Experience of racism – which has an adverse effect on indicators of both mental and physical health.
- Refugees and migrants do not prioritise their healthcare needs compared to other primary needs such as immigration issues, housing and employment – and as a result they are often late in seeking healthcare, have poor uptake of prevention services, etc.

---

115 For a review of the issues and a comprehensive set of recommendations, see Commission for Patient and Public Involvement in Health (2006) *Unheard Voices – Listening to the Views of Asylum Seekers and Refugees*.

- HIV and sexually transmitted infections, and other communicable diseases such as TB, are common in Sub-Saharan African refugee and migrant communities, yet there is often stigma or other barriers towards people seeking help with them.

Who is responsible for ensuring equality of access to healthcare?

Nationally, the National Health Service (NHS) and, in England, the Primary Care Trusts (PCTs) are responsible for equality of access to healthcare. The PCTs are the guardians of their local population's budget for the provision of health services free at point of delivery, regardless of ability to pay.

At the moment PCTs deliver community services, manage GP contracts and buy or commission acute hospital and mental health services. This will no longer be the case in the future. PCTs will instead be in charge of deciding which organisations should provide each local health service for the local population. The PCT will be free to choose, for example, between a number of NHS trusts, independent health organisations, private healthcare and voluntary and community organisations.

The NHS in Scotland is managed by the Scottish Government through 15 local health boards, which are the commissioning bodies. Community Health Partnerships (CHPs) were introduced in April 2005, but are still in various stages of development across Scotland. In some health board areas there are several CHPs. Their purpose is to strengthen primary and community-based service planning and delivery and develop joint working between health boards, local authorities, the voluntary sector and other partners. Other important bodies in Scotland include:

- *Voluntary Health Scotland* (VHS – www.vhscotland.org.uk) is a national network of voluntary health organisations which has 304 members. Its aim is to develop strategic partnerships with health services in Scotland so that voluntary and community organisations can maximise their contribution.

- *National Resource Centre for Ethnic Minority Health* (www.nrcemh.nhsscotland.com) – which supports NHS boards to develop their cultural competence in delivering health services to black and minority ethnic groups, to reduce inequalities and to improve the health of these communities.

- *The Community Health Exchange* (www.chex.org.uk/) whose remit is to support community development approaches in health services, including capacity building for local organisations.

The NHS in Wales is run by WAG through three regional offices; there are 15 NHS trusts and 22 local health boards (responsible for local commissioning). Health Commission Wales is responsible for specialised commissioning.[116]

What is practice-based commissioning?

The policy statement *Creating a Patient-led NHS*[117] proposes changing the whole system so there is more choice, more personalised care and real empowerment of people to improve their health. The Department of Health has also introduced a new policy on commissioning within the NHS.[118] It aims to devolve power to local doctors and nurses to improve patient care. It is also a way of aligning local clinical and financial responsibilities.

Under 'practice-based commissioning', GP practices will take on responsibility from their PCTs for commissioning services that meet local health needs. Commissioning practices, or groups of practices, will have four main functions:

- designing improved patient 'pathways'
- working in partnership with PCTs to create community-based services that are more convenient for patients
- responsibility for a budget delegated from the PCT, which covers acute, community and emergency care
- managing the budget effectively.

GPs will not be responsible for actually placing or managing contracts. That will be done by PCTs on behalf of practice groups.

Are there specific opportunities for third sector organisations?

The Local Delivery Plan (LDP) establishes the PCT's priorities for the year and influences the commissioning process. The intention is that third sector organisations are considered as potential service providers when new services are being developed or changed.

The PCT has also a challenging public health agenda to deliver (as outlined in the paper *Choosing Health*[119]) and wants to get the maximum input from any investment

---

116 www.assemblywales.org/nhsstructures.pdf provides a guide to structures in Wales.
117 DH (2005).
118 DH (2005) *Commissioning a Patient-led NHS: Delivering the NHS Improvement Plan*.
119 DH (2004) *Choosing Health: making healthier choices easier*.

in the third sector, as the voluntary sector plays a crucial part in working with residents to address health inequalities – especially in certain areas:

- reducing the prevalence of smoking
- reducing obesity, and improving diet and nutrition
- increasing the amount of exercise people take
- encouraging and supporting sensible drinking
- improving sexual health, including reducing teenage conception rates
- improving mental health.

From now on, investment in the third sector will need to reflect more closely the priorities detailed in the PCT's Local Delivery Plan. Third sector organisations should be in a better position to demonstrate where they can contribute to the achievement of NHS targets and healthcare priorities, including self-management and prevention programmes.

The Department of Health also has a specific policy to promote social enterprise, is running a pathfinder programme, and has a special Social Enterprise Fund.[120]

What potential exists for MRCOs?

As already described, PCTs will increasingly focus on promoting health and commissioning services and arrangements should be made to secure services from a range of providers – rather than just through direct provision by the PCT. This will bring a degree of contestability to community-based services, with a greater variety of service offerings and responsiveness to patient needs. In some types of services, there may be a range of providers – including the voluntary sector.

Many PCTs already acknowledge the crucial role that the third sector plays in delivering services, providing infrastructure support and achieving wider public participation. MRCOs in particular can argue their ability to deliver vital services – often in a less bureaucratic and more responsive way – to migrant and refugee community groups who have built a good relationship and trust with them.

Areas in which MRCOs could play a role include:

- helping newly arrived refugees and migrants to register with GPs and dentists, eg through outreach projects

---

[120] Details in the commissioning section of the DH website (www.dh.gov.uk/PolicyAndGuidance/OrganisationPolicy/Commissioning/fs/en).

- offering health assessments for HIV, TB and other communicable diseases
- supporting the registration with UK health organisations of trained refugee and migrant health workers
- securing child immunisation of asylum seekers in temporary accommodation
- providing help with mental health problems resulting from a variety of causes, such as coping with a new culture, uncertainty over asylum claims, racism or the after-effects of torture.

MRCOs could be involved at different levels of commissioning and procurement processes to ensure the effectiveness of patient-led NHS commissioning:

- *MRCOs as health-needs assessors and community researchers* – research and development or commissioning departments of the NHS could commission an MRCO to undertake community-based research on a health condition or service they think is better investigated by such an MRCO. For example, health-needs assessment and analysis within a specific refugee or migrant community, in relation to the need for diabetic services. The research would be intended to inform the commissioning process and determine whether or not MRCOs are best placed to provide the service identified or reviewed.
- *Service development/improvement* – MRCOs could work in partnership with NHS organisations to design targets, outcomes and mechanisms for monitoring and evaluation of services relevant to their communities.
- *MRCOs as service providers* – MRCOs are appropriately placed to provide certain specific services through the NHS commissioning or procuring processes.
- *Providing a person/patient focus* – this refers to the patient as a focus for effective commissioning at the various levels. MRCOs should score highly in their ability to provide patient-focused services.

NHS organisations could also help MRCOs to build their capacity to compete in the market-driven NHS commissioning process, in ways suggested elsewhere in this guide.

Some examples of services commissioned by NHS organisations

PCTs and NHS Trusts fund many one-off/time-limited MRCO-led/run projects but very few develop to a longer-term, mainstream commissioned service. Some examples that have developed into longer-term arrangements are given below (although they are not examples of the new approach to commissioning just described).

More responsive public services?

A further example is the Vietnamese Mental Health Services (VMHS – see page 125). VMHS have a joint contract from three PCTs – Lewisham, Southwark, and Lambeth, enabling the project to provide mental health services for clients who are spread across London, while minimising time spent in negotiation, assessment and other bureaucracy. They also have a separate contract with an NHS Trust.

Migrant and Refugee Communities Forum (MRCF)

The Migrant and Refugee Communities Forum (MRCF) is a migrant and refugee-led second-tier infrastructure organisation. MRCF has 13 years experience in delivering community development support, assistance and advice to migrant and refugee communities, community-based accredited training, research, advocacy, health and welfare support projects. Over the last few years MRCF has created meaningful partnerships between the voluntary and statutory sectors and immigrant community groups. At present it is running eight projects and employs six full-time and seven part-time members of staff who between them speak eight community languages.

Some of the main projects include:

- *Strategic Advocacy and Outreach Project* – providing direct casework assistance to individuals. The project provides access to five languages among staff and 15 other languages among trained volunteers. Strategic advocacy also takes casework further by working to remove obstacles to access at the level of service providers.

- *Overseas Healthcare Professionals Project* – provides employment advice and guidance, structured study groups, clinical training, financial support, professional communication and finding work training, to overseas doctors and dentists. There are currently over 1700 doctors and dentists registered with the project. In the boroughs of Westminster and Kensington and Chelsea the programme has to date supported over 60 doctors out of which 12 are now employed by the NHS and 29 are job-ready. Thirty dentists have also been supported by the programme.

- *Research and Consultations* – on health, race equality, mental health, integration, employment, etc. Reports are available on the MRCF website. Reports are used for informed advocacy and lobbying for meaningful change of practice and policy. All of these are commissioned by the PCTs, NHS Trusts and local authorities as MRCF was best-placed to undertake the research or consultation exercise.

More details, latest reports and newsletters can be found on their website: www.mrcf.org.uk

Improving access to healthcare

Naz Project London

Naz Project London (NPL) is the longest-established and largest BME-initiated and led sexual health and HIV charity in London. It exists to promote sexual health among BME communities in London. It works closely with NHS Trusts and social services especially in North West London where it is based. The services and projects are commissioned and supported by statutory and charitable organisations. NPL has 18 staff and 40 key volunteers.

NPL is a leader in providing culturally sensitive sexual health promotion and STI/HIV prevention services as well as support for people living with HIV from BME communities. In order to maximise cultural and linguistic depth of involvement, NPL's programmes target a limited number of BME communities including refugees, asylum seekers and migrants from the Horn of African, Portuguese speakers (mainly Brazilians and Africans), South Asians, and Spanish-speaking Latin Americans. NPL works across London and is developing satellite offices in selected boroughs.

NPL, in collaboration with the Trust for the Study of Adolescence, has conducted in-depth research to gain a fuller understanding of sexual health issues among young people from BME groups. The findings (available at the website below) will influence policy and service delivery.

Source: www.naz.org.uk

Other opportunities to provide health-related services may occur through local authorities. For example, the Latin American Golden Years Club in Lambeth provides health-related and other support to older people from that community and has received capacity-building support from the PCT (see www.raceforhealth.org/casestudies.php?id=7&csid=45).

What factors should MRCOs bear in mind?

There are very specific criteria used in the commissioning process which must be met by MRCOs or other bodies commissioned to provide NHS services, in addition to the criteria mentioned for all services in part one of the guide:
- clear understanding of demand-side issues and any attendant complications in the supply side (a good example could be if MRCOs have a better understanding on why refugees and asylum seekers use accident and emergency services more frequently than normal)

- understanding practice-based commissioning and related changes, eg paying by results
- core purposes and rules governing commissioning by the PCT
- evidence of local knowledge and prior experience of partnership working.

A representative of a PCT, commenting on the guide, said that MRCOs need to:

'…try to influence the commissioning process at the needs assessment/priority-setting stage because they are the organisations with the intelligence about the needs of the communities they serve, and which is in danger of being missed. This is crucial because if the needs are not recognised in the priority-setting stage then they will not be reflected in the commissioning priorities: the opportunities for MRCOs to bid will be reduced and the added value of MRCOs as service providers for these communities will not enter the equation.'

How can MRCOs find out more?

The local PCT is the first point of contact for commissioning of local health services. The local PCT website should provide information on the Local Delivery Plan and practice-based commissioning.

Other useful websites include:

Department of Health – especially the Commissioning Directorate and the Equalities and Human Rights Group – www.dh.gov.uk

Healthcare Commission – http://2007ratings.healthcarecommission.org.uk/homepage.cfm

Care Services Improvement Partnership – web pages on the NHS commissioning framework at http://kc.csip.org.uk/about.php?grp=462

London NHS Trusts – www.london.nhs.uk

London NHS Confederation – www.nhsconfed.org

London Health Commission – www.londonshealth.gov.uk

The King's Fund (the national 'think tank' on health issues) – www.kingsfund.org.uk

Most of the background documents on NHS commissioning can be downloaded from the Department of Health website (www.dh.gov.uk). The key ones are:

Commissioning Framework for Health and Well-being. March 2006.

Commissioning a Patient-Led NHS. July 2005.

Implementing Payment by Results: Technical Guidance 2006-07 (Executive Summary). January 2006.

Our health, our care, our say: a new direction for community services. White Paper. January 2006.

Choosing Health: making healthier choices easier. November 2004.

Commissioning an 18-week Patient Pathway: Proposed Principles & Definitions – A Discussion Document. October 2005.

Practice-based Commissioning: early wins and top tips. February 2006.

National Service Framework for Children, Young People and Maternity Services. September 2001.

National Standards, Local Action. 2004.

Chapter 14

Legal Advice Services

> **What this chapter is about**
> - what the services are
> - opportunities for bidding for legal advice services
> - special provisions for third sector organisations
> - special provisions about BME-related services
> - potential for MRCOs and examples of MRCOs as service providers
> - factors to be kept in mind and brief summary of requirements
> - where to get more information

What are legal advice services?

Many MRCOs provide advice on areas such as housing, welfare benefits, employment, asylum and immigration issues, consumer problems and debt, etc. Advice on all of these requires knowledge of the law, and organisations seeking funding for such services may be asked to provide proof that staff or volunteers know enough about the law to give advice to the appropriate level.

The levels of advice offered are usually defined as:

- *information services* – telling people about their rights and options
- *casework* – working with the user over time, writing letters, arranging meetings, etc
- *representing* users at review panels, appeals, tribunals or in the courts (for some courts this has to be done by a lawyer or barrister).

Grant funding is available for these services, where funders are convinced that they are needed, well-managed and represent value for money. However, this section of the guide is specifically about providing casework or representation services for people needing help with the law, and the options for winning contracts to provide these, from central and local government agencies.

What opportunities are there for bidding for legal advice services?

The Legal Services Commission

The Legal Services Commission[121] is a government body sponsored by the Ministry of Justice. It is responsible for legal aid in England and Wales (for Scotland, see below) and for ensuring that people get the legal advice and help they need. They have a head office in London and a network of regional offices (more details at www.legalservices.gov.uk).

Legal advice services are the responsibility of the Community Legal Service,[122] and they offer contracts for legal assistance across England and Wales. They also award the 'Quality Mark,' the quality standard for such services often demanded by funders, see below. The need for legal assistance is assessed by periodic exercises conducted by Regional and Local Community Legal Service Partnerships, which include solicitors, local authorities and advice agencies. Contracts for legal assistance at a specialist level (complex matters in specific areas of law involving the full range of legal services, including representation where permitted, known as 'civil legal aid') are then awarded by the Legal Services Commission. These contracts are only offered to solicitors or not-for-profit organisations that hold the Quality Mark at the Specialist level (see below). The Commission estimates that 625,000 new cases funded by them in this way were started in England and Wales in 2005/6.

All current Legal Services Commission contracts were due to end in 2007, and in many areas the Commission will be awarding new contracts to providers that meet their requirements. However, they are changing the ways in which civil legal aid is offered and procured, developing 'Community Legal Advice Centres and Networks' and 'Preferred Suppliers'. While these processes will not be complete until 2009, they will affect which contracts are granted in some areas from before then, and may offer some limited opportunities for subcontracting.

Community Legal Advice Centres and Networks

The Legal Services Commission is looking to develop Community Legal Advice Centres and Networks in partnership with local authorities, with significant funding provided by both partners (£3m total in the case of Leicester, for example). They have already agreed this with Leicester and Gateshead councils as pilot projects for new centres, and invitations to tender for centres and networks in other areas were

---

121 The Legal Services Commission is also known as the LSC, but in the guide this abbreviation is avoided so as not to confuse the Commission with the Learning and Skills Council (abbreviated to LSC).
122 The Criminal Defence Service arranges legal advice and representation for those under police investigation or facing criminal charges.

announced through 2007. Information on these tenders is available on the Commission website.

The centres will provide access to the full range of services from advice through to representation in core social welfare, children and family legal problems. Some may include other areas such as immigration and asylum. Existing providers of legal assistance in the area will be invited to bid to run the centres, and may form consortia to do so, or set up joint ventures, because the centres are to be run as single organisations. Centres can subcontract but this must be specified when they bid because the subcontractor will also be assessed for quality, value for money, good management structures, etc. Bidding is invited from not-for-profit agencies, solicitors' firms and commercial organisations that have a track record in providing legal assistance in at least some of the relevant areas, together with sound management systems and quality accreditation.

The Community Legal Advice Networks are at an earlier stage of development, and details about how they will work and how they will be funded are much less clear.

Preferred suppliers

The Legal Services Commission has also announced that it expects to have reformed completely the ways in which it awards legal services contracts by 2009. By then, contracts will only be offered to 'preferred suppliers' who must offer:

- a good history of compliance with existing legal aid requirements
- value for money
- a soundly financed and sustainable business
- a good quality of legal advice.

This strategy is designed to lead to a smaller number of larger or strategically important suppliers. The Commission has also expressed its concerns about the performance of not-for-profit agencies compared with other providers, in particular because their costs per case are significantly higher than those of solicitors. The current arrangements for payments for not-for-profit agencies are different to those for solicitors, but this is likely to change. Advice agencies will almost certainly have to form consortia or partnerships to become preferred suppliers. Once a provider is a preferred supplier, however, the bureaucracy currently associated with running a legal aid contract will reduce considerably.

Local authorities

Most local authorities in England fund advice services via grants, although they are increasingly looking to put these within a commissioning framework and offer service level agreements (SLAs) that include many terms similar to those in contracts, including defined outputs or outcomes. They offer contracts only where there is a legal requirement that they provide a legal advice service, and otherwise offer grants for any work where they do not (partly because contracts may involve the charging and payment of Value Added Tax). Commissioning frameworks generally are developed as a result of needs assessment, then an invitation is issued to apply for grants, and SLAs are developed, with reviews determining whether funding is renewed at the end of the grant period. Organisations will have to satisfy the authority that they have appropriate arrangements for governance, financial management, quality assurance and the maintenance of expertise.

One area in which local authorities in England and Wales have a legal obligation to ensure that a service is provided is advice to those in housing need or homeless. The law also allows local authorities to offer grants and assistance to voluntary organisations to help homeless people, but some authorities prefer to offer contracts. Similar legislation applies in Scotland.

Legal Aid in Scotland

The Scottish Legal Aid Board (SLAB – www.slab.org.uk) is responsible to the Scottish Government for managing legal aid in Scotland and for innovations in service delivery (for example, recent pilot community-based advice services). Scope for new refugee or migrant-related services in Scotland may be limited, however, as there is already a well-established Refugee Legal Project funded by Glasgow City Council and the Scottish Government.

Are there specific opportunities for third sector organisations?

Both local authorities and the Legal Services Commission stress that they are keen for third sector organisations to bid for the legal advice services for which they invite tenders. Currently (although this will change) the Commission has separate arrangements for not-for-profit organisations, which allow them to tender on the basis of hours offered rather than cases started, although some voluntary organisations have chosen to apply for solicitor contracts because they offer a wider range of specialist work. As noted above, the proposed new arrangements may make it more difficult for smaller third sector agencies to get contracts unless they bid via partnerships, consortia or networks.

Local authorities have tended to look to the third sector to provide advice services, but to pay for them via grants. Where contracts are offered they may cause difficulties for the organisations involved.

> ### Example of difficulties with commissioned services
>
> A well-established voluntary organisation in London offers a range of services and has contracts with local authorities to provide some of them. One is a basic welfare benefits advice service offered in a community language but they find it very difficult. The worker is part-time, and the agency receives £15,000 annually, which does not cover overheads. The adviser is very popular in the community and sees 30 people a week, but often has to turn people away. Because he has so little time, he has to refer a lot of cases on to solicitors, even though he could deal with them. The agency would like to apply for the Quality Mark for the service, upgrade it and use that to expand the service, but cannot find the time to do the paperwork which the adviser finds quite daunting: it requires a high level of fluency in English and a good knowledge of lots of UK systems. The contract also causes some cash flow problems, and they point out that a smaller organisation would find this particularly difficult.

As local authorities develop Local Area Agreements (see chapter 3) there may be more moves to commissioning within frameworks established by the LAAs.

Are there specific opportunities for BME organisations?

The Legal Services Commission has no specific arrangements to offer contracts to BME organisations, but encourages Community Legal Service Partnerships to consider the needs of BME communities when developing their plans.

Local authorities should consider the needs of BME communities as part of their race equality strategies, and also review all their contracting arrangements to ensure that local communities are getting a fair share of what is on offer.

What potential exists for MRCOs?

It is likely that there will be little potential for new refugee and migrant organisations to get contracts directly from the Legal Services Commission in the near future, for the reasons outlined above. Indeed, existing third sector organisations are concerned that they may lose their current contracts. However, there may be possibilities via the Community Legal Advice Networks once they are developed, and they may be able to subcontract with organisations developing bids for Community Legal Advice Centres, although they will have to pass the stringent tests mentioned earlier.

There is a great deal of potential for MRCOs to get grant funding from local authorities and they may also be able to tender for the small amount of advice work for which authorities offer contracts, especially since they can often show that their communities are poorly served by other arrangements. It is important, however, to do the research: not simply state the need, but also find out which organisations may already be working in the field. This may open up options for partnerships or outreach work rather than direct service provision.

An emerging area of interest and concern is 'financial inclusion': covering money advice, debt, consumer issues and welfare benefits. There is a lot of evidence that migrant and refugee communities suffer disproportionately from financial exclusion, and there may be contracts on offer in these areas soon. These may be from the Commission, local authorities, or as subcontracts from agencies that have secured contracts themselves.

In all cases, MRCOs will have to demonstrate their ability to provide an excellent advice service in order to compete for contracts: this is looked at below.

Are there examples of MRCOs providing legal advice services through contracts?

Very few MRCOs currently provide legal advice services in this way. One that does is the Migrants Resource Centre.

Migrants Resource Centre, Pimlico

The Migrants Resource Centre has had a contract with the Legal Services Commission to provide immigration advice since 1998. It has passed all the audits and other requirements since then. The contract funds one adviser, who has the experience to act as a supervisor at Specialist level under the Quality Mark, and an administrator. It specifies the number of hours they should provide and last year they only made 85 per cent of the contract: the reasons for this are a good example of the problems MRCOs face with legal advice contracts:

- The contract did not allow sufficient time for the worker to study for or take the exams for the accreditation scheme (although he passed them).
- The organisation has gone through a series of changes and mergers with smaller organisations, all of which have left it in a stronger position. It is run, however, on a model of participatory rather than authoritarian management, and these processes demand the involvement of staff in consultation and decision-making, leaving less time for casework.

→

- The service is accountable to the community, and so it is difficult to turn people away, even if their cases do not attract funding. People may have complex cases, but advice for them is normally restricted to a total of five hours (although there is provision to apply for extra time). Clients do not stop turning up after the five hours allocated, but there is nowhere else to send them.
- The Commission is felt to be inflexible about how it grants legal aid, although there is an appeal mechanism. Some clients have had cases judged to be 'without merit' and so could not be funded. The adviser believed they were winnable, the clients have found the money to pay a barrister, and have won the case. Even then, the cases cannot be funded under legal aid rules.

The MRC is very concerned about developments in the Commission's funding scheme, the move to preferred suppliers and related proposals. It hopes to bid for the opportunities, but sees them as really intended for national organisations and private companies. The MRC hopes that it can also participate in consortia or partnerships with other advice agencies to be able to bid for contracts.

More details: www.migrantsresourcecentre.org.uk/

What factors should MRCOs bear in mind?

If MRCOs want to apply for contracts, they need to establish themselves as advice agencies. By becoming involved in local advice networks or forums they put themselves on the map and may find themselves consulted about emerging needs that they can later bid to meet. These networks and forums may also be the basis for consortia or partnerships to bid for bigger commissions. It may also be possible to work in partnership with more established agencies which will then allow, for example, staff to get the level and type of experience necessary to be able to bid for contracts later.

MRCOs might also want to consider getting involved in the relevant national advice network, advice[UK] (see below). As well as offering networking, training and information, they offer extra tailored services such as insurance and may give specific support to BME organisations in some regions.

As in all other areas, contracts are often complex to run and to monitor. Because MRCOs may be offering other advice services, some of which may be grant-funded, there is the risk of double-counting (charging the same service to two or more funders) which is more difficult to sort out in smaller organisations with fewer margins.

Contracts can play havoc with cash flow, although the Legal Services Commission will make payments in advance. Some contracts involve considerable risks, especially where decisions may be devolved to the provider, but the contractor retains the right to reclaim money if the decision is wrong.

Advice contracts may have stringent eligibility conditions: those from the Commission certainly do, with a means test, a merits test and a limit on the amount of advice that can be offered. This does not sit well with services that are run by and for the community, because users and even management committee members may not be happy with decisions to restrict services. If the organisation decides to use other resources to help people who do not get legal aid funding or whose funding runs out, they may face a growing demand which they cannot meet. The legal aid contract will ensure that they have a good reputation, so more people will want the service, which could make the problem even worse.

What requirements will they face?

Many funders and contractors insist that advice providers have or work towards getting the Community Legal Service (CLS) Quality Mark at the relevant level.[123] For example, the Legal Services Commission will not offer contracts at present to any agency that does not have the Quality Mark at Specialist level (SQM). In addition, if immigration or asylum advice is offered, the service must be registered or exempted with the Office of the Immigration Services Commission (OISC), and a failure to do this is a criminal offence. The OISC standards are linked to the Quality Mark levels.

The Quality Mark seeks to ensure that good quality advice is offered by specifying how the organisation is run, what policies and procedures should be in place and the level of experience or supervision an adviser should have. Applying for it involves not just those providing advice, but all those who manage or run the organisation.

The Quality Mark is awarded by the CLS. Unfortunately, at present the CLS is not dealing with applications for the audits necessary to get the Quality Mark unless they are from existing suppliers, organisations whose funding depends on getting the Quality Mark, or from organisations seeking to get the SQM where there is a need for more capacity at that level in that area – and even this is subject to resources. They are proposing eventually to pass the auditing to another organisation which is likely to charge. If MRCOs face problems getting audited they should raise it with their advice network or the Advice Services Alliance (see below).

---

123   See the booklet *Step by Step guide to the Quality Mark* (downloadable at www.legalservices.gov.uk/docs/quality_mark/stepbystep(1).pdf).

MRCOs may of course meet OISC requirements and achieve the Quality Mark without having commissioned contracts. For example, the East European Advice Centre in London (www.eeac.org.uk/) is authorised by the OISC and has had the Quality Mark since 2004. Other examples are given on pages 83 and 84.

How can MRCOs find out more?

The Legal Services Commission website at www.legalservices.gov.uk includes information about the Community Legal Service where all new tendering opportunities are advertised, and the documentation about the Quality Mark can be found. The site has links to local Community Legal Services Partnerships, which may also have information about other local advice networks.

The local authority website for your area will have information about advice services, usually in the 'community' section.

Advice[UK] is the national network for independent advice agencies (see www.adviceuk.org.uk).

The Advice Services Alliance is the umbrella body for all independent advice networks in the UK, including advice[UK]. It runs a CLS support service for organisations applying for or running legal aid contracts or seeking the Quality Mark. The service is free to organisations in member networks or available on subscription (£25 a year for small organisations – see www.asauk.org.uk).

The Office of the Immigration Services Commissioner (www.oisc.org.uk) regulates immigration advice: details of how to get exemption are on its website.

Chapter 15

Helping Young People

What this chapter is about
- Connexions and what it does
- how Connexions delivers services
- Connexions in transition
- opportunities for third sector and BME organisations, and for MRCOs
- examples of MRCOs as service providers
- factors to be kept in mind
- where to get more information

What is Connexions?

Connexions is a service funded by the Department for Children, Schools and Families (DCSF) and provides a co-ordinated youth support service to address problems and issues faced by young people aged 13-19 (up to 25 in the case of disabled people). In particular, it concentrates on young people identified as 'not in education, employment or training' (NEET), between the ages of 16 and 18.

As explained below, the service is in transition, as it is now the responsibility of local authorities.

The target to reduce the proportion of 16-18 year olds NEET is the primary focus for the service and is delivered mainly through support, advice, guidance, brokerage and advocacy by personal advisors (PAs), who act as a single point of contact for an individual young person. The service brief is to provide a service to all young people, including careers advice and guidance, as well as providing more intensive and targeted support to those most at risk of becoming NEET.

Connexions also undertakes specific work which tackles issues relating to:
- teenage pregnancy
- school attendance

- attainment pre- and post-16
- care leavers
- young offenders
- young people with a substance misuse problem
- homeless young people
- refugees and asylum seekers
- ethnic minority achievement.

Connexions operates only in England: in Scotland and Wales, similar services for young people may be provided by local authorities, but commissioning opportunities are limited.

How does Connexions deliver services?

Mainstream services

Connexions is financed by DCSF to provide the following services to young people in education either by direct delivery or by subcontracting:

- advice on types of employment that will be suitable for and available to them when their education ends
- advice on training or education that might help them be suitable for that employment.

Connexions employs or subcontracts to organisations the employment of PAs who:

- are drawn from a range of professional fields
- must have, or be actively working towards, an NVQ level 4 (or equivalent) in that field and have undertaken relevant appropriate assessment framework training.

PAs can be placed in the statutory, private or third sectors, so opportunities do exist for the third sector in general and the BME and MRCO sectors specifically, as long as they can demonstrate that there is a clear role for the PA and they can deliver services to the required standards with qualified staff.

PAs' work is divided into three main areas:

- *Direct work with young people and parents/carers.* This begins with a comprehensive assessment of the young person's situation to reach a view about their level of need. This stage sometimes includes a referral to specialist agencies. The PA works with the young person to identify key issues and negotiates an action plan for change and moving forward. Information, advice and guidance is given on a full range of issues such as careers, further education, training, relationships, physical/sexual health, housing, substance misuse and placing in employment, education and training. Work is also undertaken on personal development and building self-esteem. At the same time, the PA encourages parental involvement in school/college and related decisions and may act as a mediator if relationships with parents are strained.

- *Brokerage.* Both PAs and the Connexions service as a whole have a responsibility for professional liaison to secure improved responses to and better opportunities for young people. In addition, Connexions works in partnership to jointly plan services for young people and ensure that specialist help is available where required. Importantly, referrals to specialist support are done under clear protocols and with stipulated requirements of the support agency. Connexions recognises that third sector organisations have an important role to play in delivery of a range of services which complement those provided by the statutory or private sectors (careers companies are private providers and are frequently subcontracted by Connexions) who play a role in meeting the needs of young people.

- *Review.* Connexions is geared towards positive outcomes for young people and any provider of their services must be capable of tracking progress through a tracking/information delivery system which meets the requirements of the Connexions Client Caseload Information System (CCIS). A young person's progress is monitored against mutually agreed plans and feedback from the young person themselves and other agencies involved are seen as a critical part of the process.

Assistance to young people with learning difficulties or disabilities

Connexions PAs are involved in undertaking the statutory assessment for young people with a learning difficulty and/or disability to assist them with their transition to post-16 opportunities.

Other services

In addition to the services described above, Connexions has traditionally contracted for the provision of a wider range of activities out of school hours and during holiday periods. Many of these are directed at the 'hardest-to-reach' young people and include personal development, leisure, arts, cultural and sports activities. It is in relation to this provision that opportunities for the third sector most often, but not exclusively, arise.

How is Connexions developing?

Until recently, Connexions had been delivered through regional and local partnerships. Budgets have been held at regional level (eg London had five partnerships at regional level) to purchase services at local level. All this is now changing and, in any case, how services are delivered locally has varied across the country.

The government initiatives *Every Child Matters: Change for Children* and *Youth Matters* signalled a period of change for all children's and young people's services.[124] For Connexions, the funding and responsibility for commissioning services will transfer to local authority control through children's trusts by 2008. Local authorities will develop Children and Young People's Plans and these will contain the targets for Connexions work.

At the time of writing, some Connexions partnerships continue to exist and receive direct funding and some funding has already gone direct to local authorities for the delivery of Connexions services through Local Area Agreements (see chapter 3). Whatever the funding route, Connexions services (wherever they are placed) will still be measured against NEET targets and contributions to PSA targets (those mentioned above – teenage pregnancy, and others).

What opportunities are there for third sector and BME organisations, and for MRCOs?

The first important step in identifying opportunities is to determine the current Connexions funding and structural arrangements for the area in which you are working. It is also helpful to find out what local priorities and targets have been set by the local authority within their planning for children and young people's services. These priorities and targets will determine the commissioning of services, including those under the 'umbrella' of Connexions.

Two relevant reports, *Young Black Men and the Connexions Service*[125] and *Working Together: Connexions and Asylum Seekers*,[126] recognise the importance of sensitive and culturally appropriate work with target groups. They point to the opportunities that could be created where there are significant BME communities and/or refugees and asylum seekers in a local area. Whether these opportunities actually exist will depend on local targets and arrangements. MRCOs can of course draw attention to these

---

124 Both available at the Every Child Matters website (www.everychildmatters.gov.uk/).
125 Aymer, C & Okitikpi, T (2002) Department for Education and Science.
126 Connexions (2004).

Helping young people

priority areas in making the case for Connexions services being directed at young migrant or refugee people.

A guide to the third sector and Connexions, _Connexions where it Counts_, is also available.[127] It is, however, based on the old arrangements.

The new arrangements with children's trusts and delivery of integrated services to children, young people and their families envisage close partnership working between the statutory, private and third sectors to ensure high-quality provision which meets needs, including particular needs specific to the locality and local communities.

Third sector and BME organisations need to make sure that local children and young people's partnerships are aware of their interest, if they are to take any opportunities that may arise. Third sector and BME groups can of course be commissioned to deliver services – and the detail of the arrangements would be determined locally.

Are there examples of MRCOs providing Connexions services?

Yes, there are examples, but since all the commissioning arrangements are changing, current examples will not necessarily be relevant to the new arrangements as they emerge.

Balik Arts 'Ask' Project

Balik Arts 'Ask' Project was commissioned by Connexions in 2002 as part of the local Hackney Partnership. Ask was set up to provide information and advice for young people aged 13-25, who are mainly Kurdish and Turkish. Unlike mainstream providers, in addition to standard advice and support, Balik offers its clients a wide range of related services such as radio training, film making and music training.

Balik Arts was contracted to deliver support for 60 young people and received £29k per annum.

The project reports that their other grant-funded services complement the Connexions project and provide a holistic and culturally sensitive approach to working with young people, which might not be available through more traditional Connexions outlets.

More information: www.balikarts.org.uk/

127 www.nsfund.org.uk/default.asp

More responsive public services?

One World Foundation Africa's 'Xperience' Project

One World Foundation Africa (OWFA) is a charity and limited company working in London and in Africa (Uganda) to promote the independence of the socially excluded, particularly people from the African Community and refugees and asylum seekers, living with or affected by HIV/AIDS.

Their East London based 'Xperience' project is supported by Connexions and is one of various services they provide for 15-19 year olds. The project supports young refugees, asylum seekers and people from BME communities through facilitating voluntary work placements, individual and peer support sessions, employment-related advice and signposting to information and services.

Xperience was initially funded by Connexions up to March 2006 as a pilot. Connexions then extended funding for a further 12 months. When the project was extended, OWFA decided not to target refugee and asylum seeker youths exclusively as many of the young people they were working with were reluctant to identify themselves as refugees. The policy of providing for refugee youth only 'was actually serving to exclude some young people'. Since April 2006, the project has been working with young people from a variety of BME backgrounds, around 50 per cent of them are refugees.

More information: www.oneworldfoundation.co.uk

What factors should MRCOs bear in mind and what requirements will they face?

All providers of Connexions services are required to meet their delivery standards, have qualified staff in place where appropriate (for instance, if they wish to have financing for a PA), and be capable of providing the stipulated level of client data in the correct format. In addition, it will be necessary to demonstrate that adequate performance management systems are in place in the organisation as a whole. All providers who seek funding through this stream are required to do the same.

Some of the standard requirements might be problematic: for example, one MRCO mentioned questions that were posed about sexual activities and orientation that were regarded as inappropriate in their mainly Muslim community.

OWFA (see the example above) reported having considerable difficulties in the initial stages of their Connexions project: payments were received in arrears, the system was bureaucratic and much time was spent in sorting out the finances. When the project was extended, Connexions offered a payment which was proportionally far less than the original amount. OWFA does not believe that Connexions has embraced the principle of full cost recovery. However, Connexions does now make payments in advance and OWFA says that they have been flexible in their approach in other respects.

How can MRCOs find out more?

Local authorities are the key source of information about local plans and targets. Each authority's Local Strategic Partnership (LSP – see chapter 3) must now develop a Children & Young People's Plan. Each authority also has a new structure to provide children's and young people's services which will be tailor-made to the area, so it is a question of contacting them locally or researching websites. Searching for the LSP or Children & Young People's Plan will get you there more quickly.

The Connexions website has general information about the service and some helpful publications, but nothing specifically about commissioning because this is locally managed (see www.connexions.gov.uk/).

CHAPTER 16

ESOL TRAINING THROUGH THE LEARNING AND SKILLS COUNCIL

What this chapter is about
- LSC and what it does
- opportunities for bidding for commissioned services
- special provisions for third sector organisations
- special provisions about BME-related services
- potential for MRCOs and examples of MRCOs as service providers
- factors to be kept in mind and a brief summary of requirements
- forthcoming developments
- where to get more information

What does the Learning and Skills Council do?

The Learning and Skills Council (LSC) is a non-departmental public body of the Department for Innovation, Universities and Skills responsible for planning and funding post-16 education and training (other than higher education) in England, with a budget of just over £10bn in 2006/07. In 2001, the LSC replaced Training and Enterprise Councils and the Further Education Funding Council, and now works nationally, regionally and locally from a network of 47 offices around the country.

Although the LSC funds a broad range of learning opportunities, this chapter focuses specifically on the provision of English for Speakers of Other Languages (ESOL). The LSC is the main agency funding ESOL provision for adults, although other funding sources are also available.[128] From 2006/07 the responsibility for funding, procuring and contracting ESOL provision for Jobcentre Plus customers (see chapter 17) has also been transferred to the LSC.

---
128 For example in London the LSC funds around 80 per cent of ESOL training.

In Scotland, the Scottish Government carried out a review of ESOL provision[129] and, as a result, national and local ESOL forums are being developed. Third sector provision is most likely to be delivered through a Community Learning & Development Partnership, whose aim is to 'help individuals and communities tackle real issues in their lives through community action and community-based learning'.[130]

In Wales, ESOL is funded directly by the WAG Department for Children, Education, Lifelong Learning and Skills and delivered by the Basic Skills Agency.[131]

What opportunities are there for bidding for commissioned services?

The LSC has an annual budget of approximately £8.5bn for commissioning learning provision, of which just over £2bn is provisionally allocated to fund provision for adults aged 19 and over outside the workplace.

Within this budget, addressing the needs of adults to improve their basic skills (reading, writing, maths and ESOL) in order to succeed and progress both at work and in everyday life, is a key priority. LSC funding entitles eligible learners to free tuition at entry levels 1, 2, 3 and levels 1 and 2. The LSC's priority is to increase the number of adults who can demonstrate an improvement in their basic skills by the achievement of a national test and level 1 or 2, but restrictions in funding for ESOL now mean that help for refugees and migrants is more limited than before (a briefing is available from the Refugee Council website – see appendix 2).

Another key area of third sector engagement with adult learning is First Steps Learning and Learning for Personal and Community Development, which can be used to support outreach activity that underpins community-based ESOL provision. In addition to this mainstream funding, third sector organisations have also drawn down significant amounts of funding from the LSC through other streams including European Social Fund (ESF), Local Initiatives and Development Fund, Widening Adult Participation Action Fund and Neighbourhood Learning for Deprived Communities Fund.

---

129 Available on the Scottish Government website (www.scotland.gov.uk/Publications/2006/05/11141003/0).
130 See Scottish Government (2004) *Working and Learning Together to Build Stronger Communities* (available at www.communitiesscotland.gov.uk/stellent/groups/public/documents/webpages/lccs_006029.hcsp).
131 Information on the WAG website (http://new.wales.gov.uk/about/departments/dcells/?lang=en). An assessment of the position in Wales is set out in Ci Research (2005) *Learning Insight: Asylum Seekers and Refugees*.

Are there specific opportunities for third sector organisations?

In 2004, the LSC published *Working Together, Learning Together*[132] which set out its strategy for working with partners in the third sector. The strategy recognises that the third sector is particularly good at working with 'hard-to-reach' learners and can play a role in supporting the LSC's widening participation and equality and diversity objectives. It also understands that third sector organisations can be employers, with a role to play in workforce development, and a potential source of information and expertise about communities and a channel of communication.

One of the key aims of the strategy is to open up access to mainstream LSC funds for more third sector organisations. The strategy acknowledges that at present, its funding strategy with the third sector tends to focus on short-term budgets with an emphasis on innovation. While this can produce excellent results, it also works against longer-term stability and strategic planning in the sector, sustainability for work of proven quality and coherent progression routes within the third sector and beyond, all of which the LSC wants to encourage. Opening up access to mainstream funding is seen as key to addressing this issue.

In relation to widening participation, the LSC funding formula includes an uplift factor of 12 per cent for a range of groups including basic skills learners, asylum seekers and refugees. At present, however, the LSC is operating in a difficult environment whereby it is expected to deliver greater outputs with reduced resources, in a context where demand for ESOL considerably exceeds supply.[133] Even though refugees and new migrants are recognised as groups with particular needs, and are likely to include a number of 'hard-to-reach' clients,[134] there are not necessarily any demands made or targets set for providers to reach these groups through mainstream programmes.

Most ESOL provision is currently delivered by large providers such as further education colleges, although this is sometimes then franchised to smaller organisations including those in the voluntary and community sector. For example, in 2005 around 12 per cent of ESOL provision in London was franchised from colleges to other organisations mainly in the third sector.[135] The following quote (gathered as part of the interviews for the guide) illustrates some of the opportunities and limitations involved:

> *'Franchising can be a very helpful method of ensuring outreach provision for ESOL learners who prefer to learn in non-college settings and the level of franchising serves to underline the importance of the voluntary and community*

---

132 LSC (2004).
133 See for example the Guardian report on the crisis in ESOL provision (http://society.guardian.co.uk/societyguardian/story/0,,1886566,00.html).
134 For example in the Home Office (2005) refugee integration strategy, *Integration Matters*.
135 From the draft summary of evidence for a 'Skills for Life' action plan for London, November 2005.

sector in delivering accessible ESOL. That said, colleges 'top-slice' the funding to cover management and administration costs, sometimes taking 40% of the funding.'

In recent years, an increasing number of local LSCs have begun to build positive and proactive relationships with third sector consortia. Consortia are independent and active partnerships of third sector organisations. They have different structures and ways of working but as *Working Together* explains they:[136]

> '…can shield smaller organisations from bureaucracy, simplify bidding and funding routes, facilitate the sharing of information, ideas and skills, and support curriculum development and information management. They can help with quality assurance and staff training, undertake needs analyses, and provide a strategic voice in developments affecting the sector locally, regionally and nationally.'

Underpinning the LSC remit to promote diversity, choice and specialism, the further education white paper[137] outlines how new competition arrangements will encourage new high-quality providers, enabling third sector organisations, among others, to enter the field. Smaller third sector organisations wishing to access such opportunities should therefore begin to build relationships with their local consortia in order to position themselves for the future.

The report *Skilling for Inclusion*,[138] provides further information on working in consortia in this field. Although the report focuses on working with the third sector in London, the messages apply more generally.

Are there specific opportunities for MRCOs?

The government has asked the LSC to tackle inequalities in the provision of post-16 education and deliver greater equality for all. As a consequence, the LSC is keen to work alongside those organisations that are engaged with adults who are traditionally under-represented in education and training.

Working Together recognises that BME voluntary organisations are particularly under-resourced and in need of capacity building. Work has begun to develop local and regional BME networks focusing on communications, training programmes and qualifications and quality assurance.

---

136 LSC (2004) *Working Together*, p19.
137 Department for Education and Science (2006) *Raising Skills, Improving Life Chances* (available at www.dfes.gov.uk/furthereducation/).
138 London Skills Commission (2004) (downloadable at www.cesi.org.uk/docPool/skill4inc.pdf).

Are there examples of MRCOs providing services to LSC?

So far, these are limited. A fairly large MRCO, the Refugee Women's Association, is a partner in projects supported by the LSC and also by London Councils and the European Social Fund. SACOMA, also London-based, has two LSC contracts.

RWA involvement in LSC projects

The Refugee Women's Association (RWA) is a refugee-led organisation established in 1993 to provide advice and guidance on education, training and employment to refugee women and asylum seekers. Courses are women-only, run during school hours and students are paid travel expenses and contributions to childcare costs.

RWA is involved in three LSC-funded projects:
- *Looking Ahead* is specifically for asylum-seeking women, providing general advice and guidance, referrals to other training opportunities and help with finding volunteering opportunities.
- *LORECA* is a London-wide project supporting refugees to enter training, employment and enterprise. RWA's role is strategic and (operationally) to provide capacity building to London RCOs.
- *Skein* – or Skills for Economic Inclusion Network – provides support to 3000 small community providers. RWA's role is to contribute to development of the partnership, produce a monthly e-bulletin, and to provide help and capacity building to the smaller organisations that are part of the programme.

More information: www.refugeewomen.org/

SACOMA's LSC Contracts

SACOMA (Sahara Communities Abroad) is an ethnic minority charity and limited company which owns a social enterprise, SACOMA Trading Ltd. They have nine staff as well as volunteers. SACOMA has two LSC contracts.

Their two-year (April 2005-March 2007) *Enterprising Women Project* was funded through the European Social Fund and London West LSC. One hundred BME women took part in the project through which 50 business plans were to be created and 24 women offered the opportunity to achieve an NVQ 3 in Business Start Up. Ten new businesses and six social enterprises or non-profit organisations are also to be created.

→

ESOL training through the Learning and Skills Council

> Their *London East LSC project* was also a two-year contract. The project offered training in ESOL, ICT, journalism and volunteering opportunities to sharpen the employability and business skills of 300 young BME trainees. The purpose of the training was to give learners the confidence to pursue other activities and to be independent of support.
>
> More information: www.sacoma.org.uk

What factors should MRCOs bear in mind?

MRCOs wishing to be commissioned by the LSC should:

- Find out about and join in with local or regional consortia in engaging with the LSC.
- Be able to demonstrate the needs of the communities they serve and their capacity to meet those needs.
- Be able to sell their knowledge and skills to either larger commissioned providers or to the LSC – what can you offer that others can't?
- Be aware of and be able to meet the LSC policies and procedures that ensure high-quality provision.
- Be aware that demand for ESOL at a community level tends to be from pre-entry to entry level 2, with most of this provision not directly leading to approved qualifications that contribute to the LSC's PSA target. Funding for this type of provision will therefore be much more difficult to secure.

The report *Skilling for Inclusion*[139] documents the experiences of some MRCOs in providing access to learning opportunities for excluded communities. For example, one commented that organisations going into partnership with colleges may find their services determined by targets set for the college, rather than by student needs. Another reflected that different funding bodies may use different outcome measures, a particular problem for MRCOs contracted (or subcontracted) to different commissioning bodies.

What requirements will they face?

Third sector organisations are primarily funded through contracts for service. Under this arrangement, the LSC's primary concern is with the achievement of specified outputs. The LSC can only contract with organisations that are legal entities.

---
139 London Skills Commission (2004) (downloadable at www.cesi.org.uk/docPool/skill4inc.pdf).

The LSC's approach to quality improvement is based on the principle that providers are responsible for the quality of their own services. An emphasis is placed on self-assessment and development planning, and the LSC requires all providers to assess the quality of their provision. Ultimately, quality is measured against a Common Inspection Framework through external inspection by Ofsted or the Adult Learning Inspectorate.

Main contractors are required to be accredited by LSC, and are responsible for ensuring that any subcontractors are able to deliver good quality services. This frees subcontractors from many of the administrative requirements that would otherwise exist. Nevertheless, subcontractors need to be aware of the requirements that main contractors must meet as this will affect their potential role.

The recent white paper introduced the concept of 'contestability' in relation to its mainstream provision and outlined how the LSC will introduce new competition arrangements to bring in new providers, including those from the third sector. The LSC has reviewed the basis for future funding of ESOL provision to ensure that available funds are well-targeted.

How can MRCOs find out more?

Organisations seeking to become funded by the LSC for the first time should approach their local LSC for a preliminary discussion. Starting discussions in early autumn would be necessary in order to secure access to funding by the following August. Each local office will have a dedicated person whose role is to liaise with third sector consortia.

The LSC website includes a specific third sector page (www.lsc.gov.uk/vcs) which contains an online directory of third sector learning links, a 'map' of all the known third sector consortia in England and a toolkit which supports the LSC and third sector organisations to work together.

LSC also publishes a two-volume toolkit for working with the voluntary sector, *Working Together in Practice* (which can be downloaded at www.lsc.gov.uk/publications/). It has specific guidance on issues such as capacity building and establishing consortia.

Chapter 17

Job-Related Training and Other Services through JCP

What this chapter is about

- Jobcentre Plus and what it does
- opportunities for bidding for commissioned services
- special provisions for third sector organisations
- special provisions about BME-related services
- potential for MRCOs
- examples of MRCOs as service providers
- factors to be kept in mind
- brief summary of requirements
- where to get more information

What is Jobcentre Plus and what services does it commission?

Jobcentre Plus (JCP) is the part of the Department for Work and Pensions (DWP) which is concerned with helping people to get (back) into work across the UK. It maintains local job centres – but in relation to this guide the main area of interest is its training programmes and outreach work delivered locally and aimed at different groups of unemployed people.

JCP has an annual budget of approximately £1bn for commissioning what it calls 'client-facing' services – to support unemployed people into work. These include the major New Deal programme but also smaller services such as its previous Ethnic Minorities Outreach programme (see below).

For large programmes such as New Deal, JCP commissions large contractors, but these are expected (where appropriate) to involve more specialist groups, for example through subcontracting. JCP expects a diverse range of subcontractors to be employed, reflecting diverse needs. Within their bids, contractors have to supply evidence of any agreements they have reached with subcontractors.

Are there specific opportunities for third sector organisations?

JCP is committed to providing opportunities for the third sector when commissioning services, including community-based and BME organisations. Its guidance requires contractors to show how links with third sector bodies will deliver 'community benefit', and how this will be measured. This might be demonstrated in a range of potential ways – such as reducing community conflict, reducing drug misuse, providing work placement opportunities for young people who would not otherwise have access to them, etc. Community organisations have to be able to show the principles that guide their work and how these will relate to the services they deliver. They must be able to show how the planned services relate to actual needs in the areas or communities they cover.

JCP assumes that potential third sector providers are aware of the principles of 'full cost recovery' (see chapter 9). It does to some extent ensure that subcontracts are 'third sector friendly': for example, the main contractor must agree to pay subcontractors within 30 days. If things go wrong, JCP believes that it imposes tight obligations on contractors not to leave smaller providers 'high and dry'.

Are there specific opportunities for BME organisations and MRCOs?

JCP asks contractors for information on the nature of subcontractors, including whether they are from BME communities (a point suggested as good practice in chapter 8). Contractors may therefore be particularly open to BME providers, as long as they can clearly demonstrate their ability to deliver the 'community benefits' which JCP requires.

Until recently, JCP had an Ethnic Minorities Outreach Programme aimed at tackling high unemployment in BME groups. Approaches included work with individuals (counselling, mentoring, helping them to overcome disadvantages in the jobs market) and with potential employers (breaking down barriers to the employment of people from BME communities). Inclusion of refugees and other new migrants was encouraged in the guidelines for the programme.

In principle, JCP is open to services being provided through MRCOs who may be able to relate to communities that other providers would find hard to reach. In practice, it

Job-related training and other services through JCP

deals largely with big providers who are therefore expected to involve smaller ones in addressing specific needs.

However, the DWP (unlike most other departments) does have a specific strategy for refugee services.[140] It describes the potential role of RCOs as part of local partnerships to identify and address refugee employment needs. This is part of the JCP's *Refugee Operational Framework*[141] and sets out the basis of JCP's work with refugees and refugee organisations. The framework mentions RCOs and the potential for partnership working, although its practical examples mainly involve non-RCO bodies. Even so, the existence of the strategy and the framework provides a starting point for RCOs wishing to provide services in the employment training and outreach area.

In Scotland, New Roots Scotland is a strategic partnership of agencies, including JCP, working together to support existing employability services for refugees and asylum seekers and to develop provision where none exists. The aim is to help asylum seekers and refugees integrate into Scottish society and enable them to play their full part in the economy. In 2006 New Roots Scotland was invited by the Scottish Government to develop a series of action points for the Scottish Refugee Integration Forum around education, training and employment issues.[142]

Are there examples of MRCOs providing services to JCP?

Yes, but limited so far. Here are two examples.

NETT in Sheffield

NETT (Nationwide Ethnic Transport Training) is a migrant-led social enterprise which provides training programmes for drivers (eg of LGVs and forklift trucks) under a JCP contract. It has successfully widened its remit from an initial focus on migrant communities to providing services to unemployed people more generally (while retaining the culturally sensitive focus of its services, and also having a client base of people who have found it difficult to get/retain jobs). It now has 20 staff.

Further information: www.nettraining.org.uk

---

140 *Working to Rebuild Lives* (available at www.dwp.gov.uk/publications).
141 Other documents in the framework are not available on the public part of the JCP website.
142 More information is available at the New Roots Scotland website (www.newrootsscotland.org.uk – site currently under development).

RCOs do already work in partnership with JCP in Birmingham, through RETAF (Refugee Employment Training and Advocacy Forum), although this is not a commissioned service.

> ### RETAF, Birmingham
>
> The Employability Forum has been working in partnership with Jobcentre Plus in Birmingham to help a local travel company recruit refugees to fill vacancies for bus drivers. Employability Forum seconded a member of their staff, a refugee, to the Handsworth Jobcentre to work with refugee communities locally to identify suitable recruits. Over 20 refugees registered their interest and training led initially to four being employed by the travel company. This showed that refugees can be the best advocates for demonstrating to employers the benefits of a diverse workforce.
>
> Since then, over 30 RCOs in the West Midlands have come together to form RETAF with the aim of maximising the number of refugees getting into work. RETAF works with the Employability Forum and Jobcentre Plus in a partnership which plans to involve more refugees as advocates to work with their communities, employers and Jobcentre Plus to share information and encourage greater recruitment from this group.
>
> Source: *Working to Rebuild Lives*, p22.

What factors should MRCOs bear in mind?

MRCOs wishing to be commissioned in this area are likely to need to 'sell' their knowledge and skills either to larger, commissioned providers or (possibly) as providers of limited services to local JCP district managers. Clearly they will need to be able to demonstrate their own capacity, but also the extent of (potentially hidden) need in the communities they serve. That refugees (in particular) face barriers in the jobs market is already established through research published by DWP to which RCOs can refer.[143]

Main contractors have to be accredited by JCP, but it is their responsibility to ensure that subcontractors are able to deliver good quality services. This frees subcontractors from many of the administrative requirements that would otherwise exist. Nevertheless, subcontractors need to be aware of the requirements that main contractors must meet as this will affect their potential role. The 'partners' section of the JCP website (see below) contains information on accreditation and on the quality framework within which providers must operate.

---

[143] *Refugees' opportunities and barriers in employment and training* (DWP research 179, available at www.dwp.gov.uk/publications).

How can MRCOs find out more?

JCP has a 'partners' section of its website (www.jobcentreplus.gov.uk/JCP/Partners/index.html) which contains general information and guidance on commissioning opportunities, both nationally and at more local levels.

JCP also works with the Association of Learning Providers whose website (www.learningproviders.org.uk) has an exchange facility for potential subcontractors. MRCOs with a firm interest in exploring opportunities in this area might start by looking at which similar bodies are already engaged in providing services, and what main contractors there are operating in their areas who might be approached.

London-based MRCOs can join the network created by LORECA (London Refugee Economic Action – www.loreca.org.uk). The network exists to inform and support organisations helping refugees into work.

The JCP procurement division (through discussions during the preparation of this guide) encourages MRCOs to make contact with local JCP district managers to discuss commissioning opportunities and the training-related needs of refugee and migrant communities. District managers do have some discretionary funding for addressing unmet needs which in principle might provide opportunities for MRCOs to provide services.

APPENDIX 1

KEY DOCUMENTS AND INFORMATION SOURCES ON COMMISSIONING AND MRCOs

This does not include all the documents referred to in the text, but only the main sources of information. It does not include the specialist sources listed in the different chapters in part two.

Official documents on commissioning, the third sector and aspects relevant to MRCOs

Audit Commission (2007) *Hearts and Minds: Commissioning from the Voluntary Sector* (available at www.audit-commission.gov.uk).

Cabinet Office (2006) *Partnership in Public Services: An action plan for third sector involvement* (available at www.cabinetoffice.gov.uk/third_sector/public_services/public_service_delivery.aspx).

CLG (2006) *Strong and Prosperous Communities: The local government white paper* (available at www.communities.gov.uk).

CLG (2007) *Third Sector Strategy for Communities and Local Government* (available at www.communities.gov.uk).

Commission on Integration and Cohesion (2007) *Our Shared Future* (available at www.integrationandcohesion.org.uk).

Communities Scotland (2006) *Making the Case: Social Added Value Guide* (available at www.communitiesscotland.gov.uk/stellent/groups/public/documents/webpages/otcs_014654.pdf).

Communities Scotland (2007) *Better Value: Purchasing public services from the social economy* (available at www.communitiesscotland.gov.uk/stellent/groups/public/documents/webpages/cs_017271.pdf).

DH (2006) *No Excuses. Embrace Partnership Now! – Report of the third sector commissioning task force* (available at www.dh.gov.uk).

DTI (2003) *Public Procurement – A toolkit for social enterprise* (available at www.socialenterprise.org.uk/page.aspx?SP=1652).

HM Treasury (2002) *The Role of the Voluntary and Community Sector in Service Delivery – A cross-cutting review* (available at www.hm-treasury.gov.uk).

HM Treasury (2007) *The Future Role of the Third Sector in Social and Economic Regeneration: Final Report* (available at www.hm-treasury.gov.uk).

Home Office (2001) *Black and Minority Ethnic Voluntary and Community Organisations – A code of good practice* (available at www.thecompact.org.uk).

Home Office (2004) *Change Up – Capacity Building and Infrastructure Framework for the Voluntary and Community Sector* (available from the Office of the Third Sector website www.cabinetoffice.gov.uk/third_sector/).

Home Office (2005) *Integration Matters* (summary available at www.icar.org.uk/?lid=5043).

Home Office (2005) *Strengthening Partnerships: Next Steps for Compact* (available at www.homeoffice.gov.uk/documents/2005-strengthening-partnerships/).

Office of Government Commerce (2004) *Think Smart, Think Voluntary Sector! – Good practice guidance on the procurement of services from the voluntary and community sector* (available at www.grant-tracker.org/index.cfm/section/Publications/key/070705PublicProcurement).

Scottish Government (2006) *Transforming Public Services: the next stage of reform* (available at www.scotland.gov.uk/Resource/Doc/172410/0048184.pdf).

Official websites on commissioning and on the third sector

Accounting: the government accounting website www.government-accounting.gov.uk

ChangeUp www.changeup.org.uk/overview/jargon.asp

Community interest companies www.socialenterprise.org.uk/Page.aspx?SP=1626

Full cost recovery www.fullcostrecovery.org.uk

Office of the Third Sector www.cabinetoffice.gov.uk/thirdsector

Social enterprise www.socialenterprise.org.uk

The Compact www.thecompact.org.uk

Other documents

Blackmore, A (2006) *How Voluntary and Community Organisations can help Transform Public Services* (available at www.ncvo-vol.org.uk/).

Perry, J (2005) *Housing and Support Services for Asylum Seekers and Refugees – A good practice guide*. Chartered Institute of Housing for the Joseph Rowntree Foundation.

APPENDIX 2

SOURCES OF HELP WITH CAPACITY BUILDING

The guide has emphasised the importance of MRCOs developing the different capacities they will need if they are to become providers of commissioned services. As a supplement to chapter 7 (which deals with capacity building), this appendix lists the organisations and other sources of help with capacity building, especially those particularly relevant to MRCOs.

Government-led programmes

The government strategy for developing infrastructure organisations is called ChangeUp and it also has a specific fund called Futurebuilders:

ChangeUp
ChangeUp is a government strategy, with funding of £150m over four years, aimed at improving the capacity of the third sector, run by an agency called Capacitybuilders. Its main role is to create 'hubs' of expertise at national and regional levels (in England only), covering the main areas in which capacity building is thought to be needed. Local third sector infrastructure bodies are drawing up Local Infrastructure Development Plans. Developments can be followed on the ChangeUp website (www.changeup.org.uk/overview/introduction.asp), and through a quarterly newsletter.

MRCOs have so far been little involved in ChangeUp – one issue for them is that it is based on local authority boundaries whereas MRCOs may straddle different authorities. Another is that ChangeUp may be oriented towards long-established BME groups rather than newer ones.[144] Capacitybuilders has a specific programme, 'Improving Reach,' aimed at capacity building for marginalised groups, of which MRCOs are one category.

Futurebuilders
Futurebuilders works proactively with local authorities to help improve dialogue between third sector organisations and public sector purchasers and

---

[144] For example in the West Midlands, a study for the Refugee Strategy Network found a number of obstacles to RCOs accessing ChangeUp programmes. See CSK Strategies (2006) *Commitment to Change: Improving Access to Third Sector Infrastructure for Frontline Refugee Organisations*. Refugee Council.

commissioners. It actively encourages commissioners to identify and refer organisations they would like to contract with, and who they feel would benefit from a Futurebuilders investment. Often the organisation in question requires capacity-building support to enable it to successfully bid for, and win, public sector contracts. In such cases Futurebuilders may offer the organisation a development grant to help it build this capacity, with the expectation that it will return for a full investment at a later stage.

For example, the Bangladesh Youth & Cultural Shomiti was awarded a £19,933 development grant to support a scheme based in the disadvantaged neighbourhood of Highfields in Leicester, working towards equipping Bangladeshis with English language and IT skills. The grant will be used to analyse governance, management, service delivery and financial planning, and recommend a strategy for enhancement. It will also help the organisation to identify and negotiate with purchasers and produce a realistic budget and cash flow.

Futurebuilders also encourages applications from consortia, and often awards development grants to provide consortia with capacity-building support. For example, it is currently supporting ten consortia, through development grants, to help them secure contracts with the Learning and Skills Council (LSC).

The limitations of both ChangeUp and Futurebuilders at local level are considered in the recent Audit Commission report *Hearts and Minds: Commissioning from the Voluntary Sector* (see appendix 1).

Infrastructure organisations

A range of organisations provide capacity-building services or support at national level, such as:

ACBBA (Association of Community-Based Business Advice) –
www.acbba.org.uk/

ACEVO (Association of Chief Executives of Voluntary Organisations) –
www.acevo.org.uk

advice[UK] – formerly known as FIAC – support for independent advice centres –
www.adviceuk.org.uk/

Charities Aid Foundation – www.cafonline.org

Charities Evaluation Services – http://www.ces-vol.org.uk/

Appendix 2

NAVCA (National Association for Voluntary and Community Action) – www.navca.org.uk

NCVO (National Council for Voluntary Organisations) – www.ncvo-vol.org.uk

SCVO (Scottish Council for Voluntary Organisations) – www.scvo.org.uk

Social Enterprise London – www.sel.org.uk/

Organisations specific to BME groups

AWEMA (All Wales Ethnic Minority Association – www.awema.org.uk) – see page 51.

BEMIS (Black and Ethnic Minority Infrastructure in Scotland – www.bemis.org.uk) – see page 51.

BTEG (Black Training and Enterprise Group – www.bteg.co.uk) – has a range of sector development programmes for London-based BME groups.

CEMVO (Council of Ethnic Minority Voluntary Sector Organisations – see case study on page 80 and www.cemvo.org.uk) offers capacity-building services to BME organisations in England, Scotland and Wales. Its 'Interface' project, supported by ChangeUp, is targeted at MRCOs and other groups that have capacity-building needs which may not have been met by other programmes.

EBSP (Ethnic Business Support Programme – www.ebsp.org), sponsored by the Welsh Assembly Government.

Specialist bodies for MRCOs

Among the bodies that specifically assist capacity building in RCOs and/or MCOs are:

CAP Research and Consultancy Ltd (www.capresearchandconsulting.com) provides finance training to people working for RCOs, leading to accreditation.

Evelyn Oldfield Unit (www.evelynoldfield.co.uk) a refugee-led capacity-building agency which provides professional support and training to RCOs.

Joint Council for the Welfare of Immigrants (www.jcwi.org.uk) provides training to allow organisations offering legal advice to achieve OISC requirements (see chapter 14).

Migrant and Refugee Communities Forum (MRCF – www.mrcf.org.uk) is a migrant and refugee-led infrastructure organisation offering capacity-building support (see page 134).

Migrants' Rights Network (MRN – www.migrantsrights.org.uk) aims to support migrant community organisations by helping them to represent themselves more effectively at all levels.

MODA (Migrant Organisations' Development Agency – www.moda.org.uk/organisation/) provides training and capacity building to migrant and BME organisations across London.

Praxis (www.praxis.org.uk) helps new residents integrate in the UK. It runs courses and provide resources and activities aimed at MRCOs, including the RCO Development Project.

Refugee Action (www.refugee-action.org.uk) provides support, development and integration work to refugees and their community organisations with services including capacity building, community relations, inclusion, awareness raising, and developing partnerships and links. It has offices in Manchester, Liverpool, Birmingham, Leeds, Leicester, Nottingham, London and Bristol.

Refugee Council (www.refugeecouncil.org.uk) provides a range of services including support to a wide variety of organisations, including RCOs and other agencies and communities who work with, support and help refugees and asylum seekers. In addition to their headquarters in London, they have regional offices in Ipswich, Leeds and Birmingham.

Refugee Voice Wales (www.refugeevoicewales.org/) is an umbrella organisation which represents RCOs in Wales. It is actively engaged in capacity building, developing services and representing refugee and asylum seeker concerns.

Refugee Women's Association (RWA – www.refugeewomen.org) helps London-based RCOs develop business skills (see chapter 15 for more information).

Renewal (www.renewalsrb.org.uk) is a capacity-building organisation for refugee groups in West London, which also offers quality assurance assessment.

RISE (www.unltd.org.uk/template.php?ID=55&PageName=rise:refugeeawards scheme) has been set up with Home Office funding to assist refugee entrepreneurs.

Scottish Refugee Council (www.scottishrefugeecouncil.org.uk) runs the Framework for Dialogue (jointly with Glasgow City Council) which aims to help RCOs engage with service providers. (SRC is further developing its capacity-building work at present.)

Welsh Refugee Council (www.welshrefugeecouncil.org/) aims to deliver a targeted range of second-tier services to RCOs and others working with refugees and asylum seekers. It has offices in Cardiff, Newport, Swansea, and Wrexham.

The Refugee Council and Refugee Action (details above) have a five-year, England-wide project, starting in 2007, to strengthen the capacity of RCOs and enhance their financial sustainability. The project will deliver customised support and training for RCOs, second-tier infrastructure organisations and funders through twelve support workers based across England.

Under Home Office proposals made in 2006,[145] there will in due course be a new capacity-building advice service for RCOs in England, delivered locally.

At local level, a range of organisations exists – such as the Northern Refugee Centre (www.nrcentre.org.uk – covering South Yorkshire), North of England Refugee Service (NERS – www.refugee.org.uk) and the Regional Refugee Forum North East (www.refugeevoices.org.uk) based in Newcastle. These offer support and training which may be relevant to organisations that want to become commissioned service providers (but much of it is oriented towards newer MRCOs who are getting started).

Further sources of general information on MRCOs are the websites of the Information Centre for Asylum and Refugees (ICAR – www.icar.org.uk) and of the Leeds-based Refugee Access project (www.refugeeaccess.info).

Public sector funders and commissioning bodies

Local authorities and other commissioning bodies may have staff with dedicated time for capacity building, or they may provide or finance training. There may also be scope for skill exchanges or secondments. Many local authorities have local Compacts for involving the voluntary sector, and these may cover the issue of capacity building and resources for carrying it out. These may be particularly targeted at BME organisations, under the BME code of practice.[146] One department may have specific responsibility, perhaps with dedicated staff, for dealing with the third sector, and these could be a good point of contact for MRCOs. In the health sector, the Department of Health has

---

145 Home Office (2006) *A New Model for Refugee Integration Services in England*.
146 See chapter 3 (and www.thecompact.org.uk).

a programme for encouraging social enterprises to develop so as to provide commissioned services.[147]

Part two of the guide contains further guidance on sources of help for capacity building in particular sectors.

Local sources of help

Regional or local infrastructure organisations exist to support and develop third sector organisations such as MRCOs. NAVCA (see above) can supply information on ones that will help in a particular region or area (email: navca@navca.org.uk or phone 0114 278 6636).

Local voluntary service councils or equivalent organisations may have general capacity-building services. In relation to the local Compact, there may be particular services or training networks for building the capacity needed by service providers. There are also opportunities locally through regeneration programmes, such as New Deal for Communities and the Housing Market Renewal Pathfinders (in parts of the north of England and the Midlands).

Other local voluntary bodies may be willing to help with capacity building. This can be informal or through more formal networks or perhaps through 'benchmarking' (systematic performance comparisons between similar organisations). It may be brokered or co-ordinated by an umbrella body (eg a local refugee forum) or by an established third sector infrastructure body such the local voluntary service council.

Web-based sources of detailed guidance

There are web-based sources of more detailed guidance and information on each of the six elements of capacity detailed at the start of the chapter:

Governance: www.governancehub.org.uk has information to help trustees of third sector organisations to build governance capacity and enhance their skills.

Workforce Development: www.ukworkforcehub.org.uk/ has information and news on skills development and good employment practices.

Performance Improvement: www.performance-improvement.org.uk has guidance for bodies offering support to the third sector to help improve the quality and quantity of what they offer.

---

147 Details of the social enterprise pathfinder programme are on the website (www.dh.gov.uk).

Finance: www.cafonline.org/policy has guidance on commissioning, fundraising and social enterprise.

ICT: www.icthub.org.uk/ has ICT guidance, good practice, advice and support for voluntary and community organisations, accessible at a local level.

Volunteering: www.volunteering.org.uk and www.volunteerscotland.info/ have a range of resources for anyone who works with or manages volunteers as well as for those who want to volunteer.

Overall support material is available from a special NCVO website (www.hubs.org.uk) and from the ChangeUp website (see above).